ISBN: 978-1-917731-02-7 (hardcover)
ISBN: 978-1-917731-01-0 (paperback)
ISBN: 978-1-917731-00-3 (kindle)

For enquiries regarding permissions, please contact:
Brand Story Publishing Ltd

Disclaimer

The views, thoughts, and opinions expressed in this book are solely those of the individual authors and do not necessarily reflect the views of Brand Story Publishing Ltd or any affiliated parties. Each author is responsible for the accuracy, authenticity, and legality of their own contributions, including any real-life experiences, personal stories, or opinions shared.

While efforts have been made to ensure that all content is presented with integrity and respect, Brand Story Publishing Ltd make no representations or warranties regarding the completeness, reliability, or accuracy of the material contained herein. Any names, locations, or identifying details are the responsibility of the individual authors.

This book is intended for informational and inspirational purposes only. It does not constitute professional, legal, medical, or psychological advice. Brand Story Publishing Ltd disclaim any liability for any errors, omissions, or consequences arising from the use or interpretation of the content. Readers should seek appropriate professional guidance where necessary.

By engaging with this book, readers acknowledge and accept that Brand Story Publishing Ltd and any affiliated parties are not responsible for any claims, disputes, or legal matters arising from the contributions of the individual authors.

START OVER

TURN ANY LOSS INTO A SENSATIONAL COMEBACK

VOL 01

14 Remarkable Authors Reveal their Powerful Journeys of Life Changing Transformation

WITH INTERNATIONAL
NUMBER ONE BESTSELLING AUTHOR

MARCO ROBINSON

START OVER VOL 1

Contents

INTRODUCTION

"Start Over

Turn Any Loss into a Sensational Comeback"

There are moments in life that tear us down so completely, we can barely see a way forward. Sometimes it's betrayal from family or friends that cuts deep, or the collapse of everything we've built – a business, a bank account, a life's work. For others, it's the quiet yet crushing trauma of abuse, or manipulation by those we trusted most. And then, for some, it's staring down the very real possibility of death.

I know, because I've been there. My story, which opens this book, isn't just about reaching a low point – it's about facing one of the most harrowing situations imaginable. There was a time in my life when I thought it was over, truly over. I found myself entangled with a Russian spy who was sent to kill me… (yes I know that sounds literally insane but read on). In those dark hours, I didn't know if I'd survive. The weight of betrayal, fear, and loss was unlike anything I'd known. I thought my life was done, that I'd come to my final chapter. But that moment, brutal as it was, became a turning point.

It was a moment that could have ended everything. Instead, it forced me to start over, to rebuild my life from the ground up, and to find a strength within myself that I never knew existed. That choice – the decision to fight back, to live, to rebuild – was the foundation for everything I am today. I used that experience to push my life in a new direction, to reach heights I hadn't imagined. And I'm not alone.

This book is filled with stories like mine – only grittier, harder, rawer. You'll read about men and women who hit rock bottom in ways you might not believe: financial devastation that left them with nothing; abuse that scarred them deeply; betrayals that cut to the bone. Some were left for dead, quite literally, by illnesses or injuries. Others were torn apart by losses that left them stripped of hope and direction. Every single one of them has faced their darkest hour and fought their way back.

The fourteen stories that follow are from warriors who have taken life's hardest blows. They've faced financial ruin, domestic and sexual abuse, narcissistic manipulation, bankruptcy, public humiliation, and betrayal. Each of them hit a point where they could have given up – and some nearly did. But instead, they chose to start over, to rise from their lowest point, and to create a life more powerful and purposeful than they had ever dreamed.

This book isn't just a collection of stories. It's a guide, a roadmap, and a call to action. The people you'll meet in these pages aren't just survivors; they're gladiators in life's arena, still battling every day to find purpose, resilience and meaning. They've transformed their trauma and pain into fuel for a sensational comeback. And through each of their stories, you'll find not only inspiration but practical steps and tools to help you take your own life from the shadows to the light.

No matter what you're facing – whether it's financial collapse, betrayal, physical trauma, abuse, or feeling trapped in a life that doesn't fulfill you – this book shows you that you can start over. You'll see how these individuals built themselves back up from the very edges of despair, harnessing their struggles to create lives of deep meaning and unshakable strength.

As you turn these pages, know that you're not alone. The warriors in this book have been there, in the depths of despair, thinking it was over. They felt the pain, the shame, the fear. And yet, they rose. They took what life threw at them and turned it into something extraordinary. Their comebacks weren't easy, but they were worth every fight, every scar, every step.

Welcome to "START OVER." This is your journey to rise, rebuild, and transform. Your comeback story starts here.

How to Read This Book and Get the Most Out of It

This isn't just a book – it's a companion on your own journey of transformation, a guide to help you unlock the strength you may not even realize you have within you. Each chapter is a testament to the power of resilience, courage, and the relentless drive to rise again.

Here's how to make the most of every page:

1. **Read Each Story with an Open Heart and Mind:** The writers in this book have shared their most vulnerable experiences – raw, powerful stories of overcoming unimaginable challenges. These are real journeys

through some of life's darkest moments: betrayal, financial devastation, physical trauma, abuse, personal crises, and more. Each story is meant to resonate deeply, offering you insight and inspiration. As you read, allow yourself to connect to the journey, knowing that this book is here to remind you that no matter where you are, there is always a way forward.

2. **Absorb the Lessons and Insights:** At the end of each chapter, you'll find a set of lessons – hard-earned truths, perspectives, and tools that the author has gained from their experience. These lessons are the keys to starting your own comeback, allowing you to tap into the wisdom of someone who has walked through similar struggles and come out stronger. Take your time with these insights, and reflect on how they can apply to your life.

3. **Engage with the Opportunity to Connect Further:** Each writer is here not only to share their story but to offer you a bridge to connect with them directly. This isn't just a book; it's a chance to build relationships with mentors who have lived through life's greatest challenges and turned them into powerful comebacks. At the end of each chapter, you'll find a QR code. Simply scan it to connect with the author and learn more from them. This is your opportunity to ask questions, seek further guidance, and even receive resources or support tailored to help you on your own journey.

4. **Take Action on Your Own Comeback Journey:** Use each chapter as fuel to inspire your own steps

forward. Whether it's a small step or a major life shift, let the stories and the lessons within them empower you to start over, to rebuild, and to create a new path for yourself. Remember, these aren't just stories of survival; they are blueprints for transformation.

5. **Reflect and Journal Your Own Thoughts and Lessons:** As you read, keep a journal nearby. Write down any emotions, thoughts, or realizations that arise. You'll likely find that these stories unlock parts of your own life journey, bringing to light the resilience you already have within. Document your journey as you read through this book – it's a powerful tool for creating your own comeback story.

This book is here to guide you, to remind you that you are not alone, and to empower you with the wisdom of those who have faced the fire and come out transformed. Embrace each chapter, reach out to any author, and let these pages be your companion as you walk your own path toward a sensational comeback.

Your journey begins now.

START OVER VOL 1

CHAPTER

1

Fallen Hero

MARCO ROBINSON

In 2019 two very bad things happened to me which left me completely broken. I didn't know if I was gonna make it through, and in fact, I actually attempted suicide. There have been two other times I have felt suicidal, one when I was a boy, when I was bullied to absolute f**k every day for four years and just saw no way out and again, when my partner betrayed me and my heart split into a million pieces. I know what it feels like to see no way out and I know what it takes to pull your life back on track, no matter how dark things get.

2019 was the worst situation I had ever been in. I was about to lose everything I had ever worked for. I was about to lose the reputation I had worked diligently to build and I was about to lose my life - all from a threat I just didn't see coming at all.

Part One

Ever slept with a Russian Spy that was sent to kill you?

The context of the following information is super important so you actually understand where I was in my life at the time. This book is intended to guide and inspire you to know that whatever situation you are in, even if you think there is nothing within your power that you can do about it… there actually is.

So to go back to the title I have written for the Prologue of this book, YES, I have slept with a Russian Spy that was sent to kill me!

I know it sounds absolutely f****g bonkers but it's the truth and I have the proof.

How the hell did my life get to this incredible precipice where it felt like I was living in a real life James Bond movie? You'll discover that in this book.

And I don't share this story to scare the shit out of you, but to let you know that very bad things can happen to very good people, and it's how you respond to those very bad things that really determines IF you get to live the dream you started this journey with in your mind or whether it stays a dream forever.

I had dreams and visions very early of what I wanted to do with my life. All of us have dreams, but very few of us actually ever act on them, because for the most part, we don't believe we *can* live our dreams. Ultimately we rarely believe in ourselves.

So let's get back to the Russian. When I was a kid of about 6 years old, I was the one at the back of the classroom staring out of the window, daydreaming the majority of my school days away.

Part of the daydream was that I was a spy, like James Bond, and I was running across the rooftops of buildings chasing the bad guys, looking very badass as I did it, and of course saving the day and winning the most beautiful woman in the world.

It was 1973, and I was influenced hugely by the Bond films at the time, especially "The Man with the Golden Gun" with Roger Moore playing Bond.

The exotic locations, mad villains and over the top storylines captivated me completely. I was there in my imagination every single day because of what was going on in my childhood at the time. It was my escape, it was the only way I knew how to escape apart from hiding under my bed to get out of the domestic violence I was witnessing every single day at home... as a child it was horrific.

Fast forward to 2016, I was 47 years old and had decided that I wanted to make my own Feature Film and star in it.

I was successful in business and I had achieved everything I wanted to achieve and really so much more than I ever thought possible, I had a successful property business, and I was speaking all over the world on how to be successful and financially free, and I had just opened my own restaurant in Kuala Lumpur, Malaysia, where I had been living since 1997.

More importantly I was well on the way to producing my own feature film and starring in it….

One day in February 2016…

Location: Naked Restaurant, Kuala Lumpur, Malaysia (my own restaurant).

I was starving and had just arrived after a super energised morning workout. I was about to order my breakfast when the phone rang.

I saw it was Adrian Bol, the co-creator & Director of the feature film "Truth99" the true story of how the Russians bombed a building in Kyiv in 1999, the film we were going to make now! (Adrian's wife was Ukrainian and lost people she was very close to in that bombing).

The conversation went something like this;

"Marco, are you sitting down?".

"No Adrian, what's up?"

"Sit the f**k down right now!"

"WHY! What the hell is up?!" I said, proceeding to sit down.

"Your face, your social media accounts, including your facebook AND your Instagram are all over Russian National News TV!" Adrian exclaimed.

"F****g BRILLIANT!" I said. "That's the best PR we can ever have for the film!"

"NO MARCO, this is not good...they have circled the comments you made in red ink about Pu**n (who we will now refer to as 'you know who') bombing that building and killing innocent people!"

"WHAT?!"

"They are saying LIVE on the news that you are crazy for making this film and you are probably not going to live very long, they said this is a dead man walking!" Adrian had said.

"Adrian, are you f***ing with me? F**k the f**k off!" I was beginning to panic.

"I'm sorry Marco," Adrian responded, "it's true, I am really sorry..."

"Adrian, this is not my film, this is YOUR film, why the f**k are they targeting me?"

"Because you're promoting it and you're the public face of the film!"

"I don't believe it! I really don't believe this..." I muttered, beginning to feel fear well up in my chest. "What the hell am I gonna do about this?"

"I don't know man, I'm in shock..."

Still not entirely believing what I'd just heard despite Adrian being a great friend and me having no reason not to trust him, as you can imagine, this was now the ONLY thing on my mind.

I reached out to Adrian and asked if we could get the Russian news story sent over to us and translated into English. I needed confirmation that this bombshell news was indeed true.

24 HOURS later I was watching the russian news article with me all over It.

Apparently it had been broadcast to over 10 million people which certainly didn't make me feel any better. I was stunned and now truly scared for the first time in my life that I was going to die a lot sooner than anticipated... the news article was true.

Seeing your own face on the news in Russia, going against the most powerful man in the world for all to see was not just surreal, it was scary as f****g sh*t, the worst kind of scared you could ever imagine in your very worst nightmares... this was serious shit and I was deep in it.

Shaken, I started calling all the people I knew, but not my family as I didn't want to scare them. I didn't want my kids to know this yct..

Fortunately, after spending some time in Ukraine auditioning actors for the film I had connected with a few Russian people and got on the phone with them as soon as I could...

To protect identities I'll just refer to my Russian friend as "Anastasia".

The phone call after sending Anastasia the news reel went like this;

"So what do you think, Anastasia?"

"I think you'll be okay Marco... I wouldn't worry about it too much..."

"Really?" I said, "have you had your face all over the national news in a foreign country and your life threatened?!"

"No! Of course not, but Russians do this a lot to sell news, I think you'll be okay. I don't want you to worry, okay, YOU WILL BE OKAY!"

And then the call ended.

Despite Anastasia's reassurance, I didn't feel ok. I felt a little better but I definitely was not ok.

You see, no one else was me... not even Adrian really understood what I was going through because it wasn't *his* face that had been plastered all over the news.

I was searching for answers and wanted to protect myself so I decided to back off for a while and not to do any PR about the film, until I felt some sense of normality and at that exact moment, normality felt like it may never be coming back!

At the same time as all of this was happening, in fact over the last 9 months, I had been talking to a stunningly beautiful Russian woman on my Instagram. We got on really well. There were voice notes and even video calls and it was going well with this girl... really well.

One day she asked to come and see me so we could meet and see how we got along in real life.

I didn't hesitate. This felt too good.

So I picked her up from the airport and sure enough we got on really well in person too.

After three days in bed… one morning she said something I did not expect at all.

And just to emphasise the gravity of this conversation, these are the EXACT words, exactly as she said them.

"Marco, I don't think you should make this film".

"Anna, why the hell would you say that?" I asked.

"Because I am not who you think I am"

"What do you mean? Who are you?"

It's silent for a few moments, and then she responds,

"I am a Russian FSB agent and I have been sent here to warn you that if you make that film we cannot guarantee your safety."

A feeling of dread begins to seep in. "What the f**k are you talking about?"

"Marco, I am a spy, I sell weapons, my best selling weapon is Cyanide, and" she reaches for her phone, "this is me and my cousin the president (you know who), you know his name."

She continues…

"Your office is bugged, your production office in Ukraine is bugged, we have been watching you and listening to you for a long time… we know what you are up to."

I was frozen with fear... how the f**k did my life come to this? What the f**k was I going to do?

F**k!

Now at the same time this was happening, I was about to be the victim of a family betrayal, a betrayal so horrific the bank came after all my assets and tried to repossess my mum's house...

And to give you context, I had just successfully recorded and broadcast my Prime Time UK Channel 4 TV Show "Get a House For Free" and given three homeless families three of my own properties. Yes I used to be homeless with my mum.

The reason I was homeless with my mum was because she had left my Dad because he was a gambling addict. She was 23 and I was 2 years old. He had accumulated so much debt she had no money to live. She had no choice.

The only place she could go was her mum's in the North of England. It was January, it was freezing cold and her mum and step father came to the door.

Her step Dad told her mum on that doorstep, "It's either me or them. They come in here and I leave. They go now, I stay." Obviously this was a very tense moment... but her mum told my mum, "I am sorry, you can't stay." Without hesitation.

I only discovered, when my mum was 70 years old, that she had been severely sexually abused by her Stepfather since she was 4 years old. When she was 12 her stepfather put his hand on her breast and said to her: "I didn't marry your mum for your mum...I married your mum to get to you."

I can't imagine how terrified she was in that moment but she lived through that abuse. She told her mum and her half sisters… they all without exception gaslighted and shamed her for even mentioning it. That's how the Patriarch was so ingrained in society, women were nothing, men were everything.

She had spent her life afraid to speak out and only told me when Channel 4 wanted my mum to share her backstory. My jaw was on the floor…

When I found out and the show came out, her sister asked me to give money to their family. My mum replied with the backstory of what her stepfather had done to her. I didn't even respond. She now had the strength to realise she should not have served that family and lived that kind of lie. It set her free.

Even before I had learned of these tragic events I had always wanted to retire my mum and ten years previously I managed to help leave her job and retire peacefully and with total peace of mind she had done the right thing by speaking out.

The reason Channel 4 had asked me to record this new TV show is because they had learned about my story when my second book was published "The Financial Freedom Guarantee - The 10 step award winning property buying system anyone can use to replace their salary, fire their boss and never work again".

They reached out to me and I didn't hesitate. They wanted to attract attention to the diabolical social housing crisis, in which it was impossible for so many people to find housing.

So we made "Get a House for Free" and I gave three properties to three homeless families. It went viral to 67 countries and changed many people's lives. I co-founded a charity subsequently and we have helped thousands of people get off the streets, find housing and get work. In fact we have a 100% success rate.

Something I am very very proud of. But now... I was about to be made homeless again... and I was about to take my own life. It was the darkest time of my life...

And I will be sharing the full details of this incredible chapter of my life in Volume TWO of "Start Over - Turn any LOSS into a Sensational Comeback"

A few last words from me...

It is through our stories that we all have the potential to live the greatest life we can and inspire others to do the same.

It is through sharing our stories that we heal and we have the power to heal others. It is an incredible gift to be able to do this and sadly many people do not have the courage to go through it as they are afraid of the repercussions, but I encourage ALL of you reading this book to rethink that stance. You can save your own life and set yourself free, and more significantly, your story is someone else's survival guide, and a guide for them to set themselves free and truly thrive...

When you share your story with a specific group of people that used to be you in the past they relate to your journey in a very special way.

They are still in their existing current story. They are experiencing a specific and unique set of problems that you have overcome. They want to be in your chapter, they want to know how you have overcome the problems they are now experiencing. This is why people with their own heroic stories of overcoming trauma, loss and adversity decide to serve those people and become coaches and consultants…

Some of the authors in this book are coaches and consultants, some just want to share their story, to help you the reader navigate through whatever challenge you are facing. I applaud every author in this book. They are remarkable because they came forward and had the courage to open up and share their stories with you, some of them for the very first time, and yes when they shared their stories many of them cried, I cried with them, but we knew as a collective group that we had the opportunity to impact many lives and do good and help people that are struggling to get to the light and help themselves. This book is for the little child in all of us who just wants to be loved and to believe that anything they set their hearts and minds can come true.

To subscribe to Marco Robinson's VIP Newsletter & receive top secret & very useful personal and business advice please scan the QR code:

ABOUT THE AUTHOR

MARCO ROBINSON

SCAN TO KNOW MORE

Marco Robinson is an international #1 bestselling author, award-winning entrepreneur, and Top #2 Netflix producer. Renowned for creating and hosting Channel 4's prime-time TV show "Get a House for Free", where he gave homes to homeless families, Marco is a philanthropist knighted in the Commonwealth for his extraordinary charity work. A three-time winner of the prestigious Two Comma Club Award for generating millions in sales, Marco has built his legacy by inspiring people worldwide to turn loss into a sensational comeback. As the visionary behind the Start Over book series, he proves that no setback is too great to overcome.

FOREWORD

To Start Over Successfully, choose the hero's journey...

What is a hero?

"The Cave you fear to enter holds the treasure you seek"

— Joseph Campbell

A hero in real life is someone who has given their life to a cause bigger than themselves.

This means you have been called to action to fulfil a deep desire. To rise from mediocrity, to stop the passive lifestyle & and actually do something meaningful with your life.

Bottom line, the quality of your life is determined by the meaning you give it and the emotion you attach to it.

Heroes embody meaning in every action they take. The emotion pours through them on their journey... they are truly "Called to Action".

You have a gut feeling that you are meant for more and you can't stop thinking about it.

You start searching for answers by asking the question you need to ask, "What am I here to do?" and the answers to that question start appearing in front of you, some you can't see, and the ones you can see, a lot you don't understand yet.

Those answers, when you decode them… when you learn their lesson, show you undeniably that you have to take responsibility for your own journey, start taking massive action and most importantly start to believe you can achieve the outcome you want.

Sometimes your calling comes through adversity and tragedy, which can be the greatest gift you will ever receive, especially if it galvanises you to take the action necessary to get what you want.

Some people start that heroic journey very early in their life because they clearly know what they want.

Some go through a kind of 'part one' of their life and suddenly realise that their own story of how they got to this present moment is meant to help others, that your story is not just somebody else's survival guide, it is their THRIVING guide.

Your story so far is full of meaning when you LEARN the lessons of the life you have already lived, as it equips you with the tools to achieve what you didn't ever think was possible and can inspire others to follow in your footsteps.

The contribution value to you when this happens can feel like one of the greatest achievements of your life, an achievement full of meaning. The epitome of lasting fulfilment. But to be a hero, you have to be "ALL IN".

People have a very different version of their idea of what exactly is "I AM ALL IN" and it is the understanding of this through your whole being that will determine if you are truly ready to pick up the "sword", learn how to use it and do battle to get what you want NO MATTER WHAT the circumstances.

If you think you are "ALL IN" just because you know it's gonna be easy and turn out right for you, you are simply dead wrong. That is not my version of "ALL IN" at all.

My version of the hero in real life, of "I AM ALL IN" is even when you don't feel like fighting for your desires, you will do it anyway, despite any circumstance, despite any challenge and despite any adversity.

I am "leaned in" to my heroes journey so far, that my mindset is programmed to learn what I don't know, yet must know to reach my goal.

If you think back to how many times you literally gave up on going for what you really wanted because it was "too hard" and you retreated into the shadows to either give up completely or re-group to figure out what went wrong (and most importantly the lesson you learned from that subjective experience) you will discover that it is only when you go ALL IN, that you will be able to overcome anything to prevail, but you won't do it when you give up and give it the meaning of "it wasn't meant to be".

The amount of times I have heard and seen that victimhood in my life is astonishing. It is the singular reason people settle for mediocrity in their lives... they are just not willing to be courageous enough to do the work necessary to win.

A strong "WHY" will overcome any "HOW"... and in this book I am going to share WHY I do the things I do and WHY other Heroes in real life do the things they do and HOW you can start doing the things necessary that you need to do to achieve your wildest dreams. And I mean it, I am a living example of if you break a goal down into small enough pieces and you have a ruthless determination to succeed when you know the meaning of your life, that is why you must make specific actions repeatedly to get what you want. If you do you will absolutely smash the f**k out of life.

The Oxford Dictionary says the meaning of a "HERO" is a person that is admired for their courage, outstanding achievements or noble qualities...

A hero in real life for me is based on the narrative of how ordinary people have experienced extreme adversity or conquered extreme goals and challenges by deciding to take that heroic journey, the journey that starts with the cave you fear to enter, by crossing an unknown threshold, to the other side which holds the rewards we all value more than anything else in this world, the sense that we have achieved something so great that we and other people had previously thought was beyond our reach.

Joseph Campbell once said, "The cave you fear to enter holds the treasure you seek." This profound statement captures the essence of a hero in real life—a person who dares to confront their deepest fears to uncover treasures of growth and fulfillment.

A real-life hero is not just someone who acts bravely in a moment of crisis; it's someone who commits to a cause greater than themselves. This journey often begins with a deep, internal calling to rise above mediocrity, to break free from a passive existence and engage in a life rich with purpose and action.

The quality of your life is defined by the meanings you assign and the emotions you embrace. Heroes infuse every action with meaning. Their emotions drive them forward, compelling them to answer the call to action. If you've ever felt a nagging sense that you're meant for more, that restless thought is the beginning of your quest.

Asking yourself, "What am I here to do?" starts to unveil answers—some clear, some obscure, all requiring interpretation. When you decode these messages, you learn that true responsibility for your journey lies in taking massive, deliberate actions and believing in the outcomes you desire.

Sometimes, our call to heroism is sounded through adversity or tragedy, revealing itself as the greatest gift. It propels us into action, ensuring we strive towards our desires. While some may embark on this heroic journey early, knowing exactly what they want, others might spend half a lifetime before realizing that their personal stories hold the power to inspire and guide others—not just to survive, but to thrive.

Your narrative to this point is laden with lessons, equipped with tools not just for overcoming the seemingly impossible but also for inspiring others to follow suit. The contribution you make by sharing your journey can stand as one of your life's greatest achievements—a testament to true fulfillment.

Yet, to truly live as a hero, you must commit completely. Understanding what it means to be "all in"—to fight for your desires against all odds and despite any challenge—is essential. If you think being "all in" means an easy path to success, think again. Being a hero in real life means fighting even when you don't feel like it, because the journey and the transformation are what matter.

In this book, I will share why I do what I do, why real-life heroes push their limits, and how you can start taking the necessary steps to realize your wildest dreams. I am living proof that if you break a goal into manageable pieces and pursue it with relentless determination, understanding the true meaning of your life, you will not just achieve but exceed your expectations.

Heroes are ordinary people who choose to do extraordinary things. They step into the unknown, confront their fears, and emerge transformed, having achieved what once seemed impossible. Now, the question remains: Are you ready to answer the call to action and be a hero in real life?

Are you prepared to risk everything to live your dream?

START OVER VOL 1

CHAPTER

2

"Deathwish

in New York"

CAMILLE WORDSWORTH

The Edge of Innocence

In my early twenties, I left behind the comforting warmth of my island home, eager to chase a world full of new possibilities. The island had been my sanctuary, its crashing waves and endless sun a comforting rhythm that felt as solid and dependable as the ground beneath my feet. The salt-laden air and the caress of the sun on my skin had been my constant companions, weaving into every fibre of my existence. Yet, a restless spirit drove me to seek something beyond the island's serene shores. I had the opportunity to study abroad—a privilege my parents proudly provided—and I was determined to succeed.

My journey took me to university in upstate New York, where I pursued my academic dreams. The campus was breathtaking in its own way—rolling green lawns, tall trees swaying in the cool breeze, and buildings that felt like they had stood for centuries. But it was a far cry from the island's raw, untamed beauty. Despite this, I could see myself thriving here, building a career, making my family proud.

But just one semester in, my world collapsed. The global recession hit like a sudden storm, merciless and without warning. I still remember the call. My mother's voice trembled, "We can't afford to pay for your school fees. " Her words cracked with the weight of the downturn that had crushed my parents' financial stability and pride. My father—always the pillar—remained silent. His silence said everything. The burden was too heavy for words.

My dreams were shattered in an instant. It wasn't their fault—how could it be? The world had changed, and we were all just victims in its wake. In that moment, my future felt like it was slipping through my fingers, and I had to face the cruel truth.

I was at a crossroads—return home to a place that offered no future or forge a path in the unforgiving expanse of New York City. I chose the latter. I had a fierce determination to prove that my journey was not in vain.

Unknowingly, this decision was only the beginning of a soul-crushing odyssey through New York's unforgiving streets.

The Unravelling

In a workplace where minorities like me often felt invisible, my journey began as a receptionist. Through relentless hard work and dedication, I was promoted to a customer service role—the first minority in the company to achieve this.

Everything seemed to be progressing smoothly until my friend, the only other minority in the company, approached me. Her eyes were clouded with frustration and sadness. She felt overlooked and discriminated against, as the company had chosen to train the boss's inexperienced niece for a managerial position instead of promoting her.

Her struggle pulled me into a moral dilemma that threatened both my job and my survival during a deep recession. On one hand, I was revelling in my hard-earned success and the recognition I had finally received. On the other hand, I was acutely aware of my friend's battle and the injustice she faced. The choice was agonising, either support my friend and risk my position in the company or remain silent and protect my emerging career. The weight of each argument tugged at my conscience with equal force.

Desperate to do the right thing but acutely aware of the risks, I approached my manager for advice. Her tone was stern and foreboding. "Getting involved could have consequences for your position here. Besides, everyone loves you! Is it worth it?" Despite her warning, my resolve to support my friend stayed unshaken.

We decided to take the matter to the owner of the small company, our only recourse in the absence of an HR department. Nervous but resolute, we arranged the meeting. My friend faltered. Overwhelmed and fearing for her job, she retracted her complaints. "I'm sorry. I don't think I really meant what I said. Maybe I was mistaken," she whispered, her voice barely audible.

I was left stunned as she denied all the issues we had intended to address. The boss turned his cold, piercing gaze on me, his disdain palpable. "So, you're the one who egged her on to make these complaints when clearly nothing was wrong?" His words felt like a physical blow, each syllable a sharp reminder of my isolated position. My face flushed with a mix of anger and shame, his scorn stripping me bare, leaving me exposed and vulnerable. The weight of his judgement and the derision in his voice made me question my own decisions and values. The cold, hard reality of my situation began to sink in as I struggled to maintain my composure.

Just as my manager had predicted, the fallout was swift and unforgiving. My job was terminated, and during a recession, finding a new one was nearly impossible. I was labelled a troublemaker, abandoned by my friend, and distanced from the colleagues who once seemed to stand by me. The betrayal and isolation were crushing, leaving me adrift in a dark abyss of unemployment and despair. This was the first sharp bend in my downward spiral. The brutality of my new reality soon deepened. Peter, my live-in boyfriend, who had been in recovery, relapsed into drug addiction.

Teetering on the Edge of Sanity

When I first met Peter on that crowded subway platform, I saw a light in him. It was like seeing a reflection of my own hope, that same hunger for something better.

His boyish charm and disarming smile felt like a beacon of warmth in the cold, harsh city. I was drawn to him—craving connection, longing for someone who could fill the void left by the distance from my island home. When he casually mentioned he was in recovery, it barely registered. I didn't understand what that truly meant, and it never occurred to me that his addiction could consume my life.

Growing up sheltered, surrounded by the protective embrace of my family and the simplicity of island life, addiction was something I had only heard about on the news—a tragic tale, but always distant. So, when Peter confessed, I didn't flinch. How could I? His words were meaningless to someone who had never lived in the storm. I was blind, ignorant of the warning signs that would soon engulf my world.

At first, I clung to the illusion of control. I thought I could save him—that if I just loved him enough, supported him enough, things would get better. It's what I knew: if you worked hard and loved deeply, you could make it through anything. Each relapse, however, unravelled that fragile hope. It wasn't all at once, but in tiny moments—each broken promise, each lie—tiny fractures appeared in the foundation of our lives. With every crack, a part of me slipped away.

I justified my choices, convinced myself that my love could fix the fissures forming between us. I stayed, thinking it would get better. "Maybe this is just a phase," I told myself, as I watched the warrior I once was begin to fade. My identity as someone capable and strong was dissolving, piece by piece. Yet, I kept fighting—fighting for Peter, for us, for some version of a future I wasn't even sure I believed in anymore.

As Peter spiralled deeper into addiction, I found myself drowning alongside him. Our finances crumbled, leaving us to rely on his mother's food stamps.

There was no pride left, no room for dignity when survival was at stake. The whispers and stares at the grocery store blurred into the background, irrelevant to the crushing weight of just getting by. But the true toll wasn't just financial—it was emotional, spiritual. Each broken promise felt like a knife, carving away at the person I used to be until I could barely recognize myself.

Yet, I suffered in silence, unwilling to burden my parents with my pain or disappoint them with the reality of my situation. I knew they would worry, and the thought of hurting them was unbearable. So, I continued to spiral down this dark path, teetering on the edge of sanity. I lost myself in Peter's addiction. Every day was a battle—not just for him, but for me. I had been strong once, a warrior in my own right, but now I felt like I was drowning in his chaos. Each lie, each choice of drugs over me, chipped away at my spirit, like water slowly eroding stone.

And then, violence made its terrifying entrance. Peter's drug-fuelled rages left me flinching at every slammed door, every harsh word. I lived in constant fear, my body tensed with the expectation of more abuse. Isolated in this nightmare, consumed by shame, I couldn't tell my parents. They were my haven, but I couldn't bear the weight of their disappointment.

The breaking point came when I discovered that my family heirlooms—rings, bracelets, necklaces passed down from my mother—were gone. Peter had pawned them for drug money. That night, something in me finally shattered. Those items were not just jewellery; they were my connection to my past, to my family, to the girl I used to be. They represented everything I had left behind when I came to this city, a tether to my heritage. And now, they were gone—stolen to feed his addiction.

Sitting there, staring at the empty jewellery box, I felt the hollowness mock me. It was a physical manifestation of the emptiness I felt inside. When he finally returned, I pleaded with him, desperate to know where my belongings had gone.

He looked at me with hollow eyes, offering vague apologies, but there was no comfort in his words. He couldn't even remember where he had sold them.

I wanted to scream, to rage at Peter, to make him understand what he had taken from me. But the words wouldn't come, and I had no strength left to confront him. Instead, I sank to the floor, trembling with silent sobs. I lied to myself, whispering that I would replace what was stolen. But deep down, I knew nothing could ever bring back what had been taken. I felt lost—disconnected not just from my past, but from myself.

Each day felt like a slow, painful descent further into darkness. I took a job selling windows, earning a humiliating $2.50 an hour plus commission. My manager, with his nimble fingers and predatory stares, took advantage of my vulnerability. His eyes followed me, lingering in a way that made my skin crawl. Every unwelcome advance, every demeaning comment, chipped away at what little dignity I had left. But I couldn't speak out. I knew it would change nothing. Girls like me—minorities, broke, invisible to the world—had no recourse. I had no voice, no power. I was just moving through the motions of life, operating on autopilot.

Then, one day, I came home to find my closet ransacked. All my work clothes, my leather coats, were gone. Peter had stripped me of my belongings once again to feed his addiction. It was the dead of winter, and I had nothing left to wear. The only option was second-hand clothes from a charity shop—thin, worn fabric that barely shielded me from the biting cold. It was a harsh reminder of how far I had fallen.

The world closed in around me, and I began to lose sight of who I was, of who I had ever been. The girl who had once stood tall, proud of her achievements, was gone. In her place was a woman barely holding on, teetering on the edge of sanity, her spirit crushed under the weight of Peter's addiction and the relentless destruction it had wrought on our lives.

I had no energy left to save myself. My only focus was Peter—his pain, his addiction, his endless promises to get better. My life became a mirror of his chaos, my identity swallowed by his darkness. Each day, I fought to hold onto whatever small thread of hope I could find, but they slipped through my fingers, dissolving into nothingness. I was teetering on the edge of homelessness. Peter's addiction consumed our lives, and I was trapped in a cycle of sleepless nights and endless worry. My family remained unaware of the full extent of my suffering, and I was too ashamed to tell them the truth. I lived in the shadows of my own life, unable to see any way out.

The Drug Gang's Predatory Stares

Peter had sold the last of my clothes before disappearing—two weeks had passed without a word. I was suffocating under the weight of loneliness and bewilderment, 'Would he ever return?' There was no one to turn to, no one who could understand the darkness I had sunken into. I remained unwilling to speak up.

Sitting on the edge of the bed, I felt lost and broken. The woman I once was seemed like a distant memory, replaced by a stranger in the mirror. I could hardly recognize myself. The warrior I once thought I was had disintegrated, leaving only a broken shadow of the woman who had left her island home full of hope and dreams.

Night after night, I sat alone in that decrepit apartment, watching myself unravel. The walls seemed alive, their cracks and stains reflecting my shattered spirit. Every creak of the floor, every faint sound outside made my heart race with dread, as I feared the next knock at the door might carry news that Peter was gone for good. I could not sleep because my mind was constantly thinking of Peter and whether he was alive or dead. Every knock or sound on the pavement outside would make my heartbeat faster. I only felt relief when he walked through the door. But this time, I feared I would never see him again.

One bitter winter night, the cold was so sharp it felt like it could slice through skin and bone. The walls of the apartment felt like they were closing in on me, suffocating me. I stumbled outside, wrapped only in a white, sheer nightgown, too numb to care about the biting chill gnawing at my skin.

As I collapsed onto the front steps, my mind drifted into a void, detached from reality, consumed by the vast emptiness around me. The world outside felt like a distant memory, and I felt trapped in a desperate existence I had created for myself.

Then unexpectedly, headlights pierced the darkness, cutting through the silence of the night. A car rolled slowly toward me, its low growl unsettling. Inside, muffled laughter and harsh voices broke the stillness, spilling out into the night. It was a car full of drug dealers—a local gang, feared and notorious. Their laughter faded as they spotted me, replaced by an eerie silence. I could feel their eyes raking over my frail, exposed form. But the danger barely registered. I sat there, unmoving, the weight of their stares heavy on my shoulders. The instinct to run, to protect myself, had long abandoned me. I had become a ghost, an empty vessel, drifting through a world where survival had lost all meaning.

What's the point? There's nothing left to save.

The car slowed to a near stop, their faces illuminated by the dim streetlights. For what felt like an eternity, we were locked in a tense silence. Their eyes scanned my skeletal frame, but I didn't flinch. There was no fear, no anger—not even shame. I was too broken to care.

Is this it? Will they take me too? Would it stop this mental pain?

I accepted my fate.

Then something unexpected happened. The men, hardened by years of violence, said nothing. They simply looked at me with a strange, quiet pity before rolling the car forward. Their gazes lingered for a moment longer before they disappeared into the night. It wasn't the confrontation I had braced myself for, but the emptiness they left behind cut deeper than any threat they could have made.

I chastised myself, I've become so pitiful that even they don't want me.

As the car vanished, I felt the weight of my reality crash down on me. In that moment, I saw myself through their eyes and understood how low I had fallen. I was barely a person anymore—just a hollow echo of the woman I once was.

Sitting there, staring at the empty street, I suddenly became aware of myself again. I lowered my gaze, taking in the translucent fabric clinging to my body, the pale skin stretched over bones that felt ready to break. I looked like a ghost, a living testament to how far I had fallen. Tears filled my eyes, and for the first time in what felt like ages, I allowed myself to feel it all—the shame, the grief, the disappointment, the overwhelming sadness. The tears came in hot, uncontrollable waves, streaming down my frozen cheeks, their warmth stark against the icy air. Each tear was a testament to the deep well of despair that had been building inside me over two years in this exhausting relationship.

But with that painful realisation came something else—a faint flicker of hope. Maybe, just maybe, I wasn't beyond saving. Perhaps there was still something left to fight for, something worth holding onto. It felt distant, like a whisper barely audible over the roar of despair, but it was there.

I'm not this. This isn't the end of me.

As I sat there, shivering in the cold, I decided—tomorrow, I would find help. I would try to claw my way out of this abyss, even if it meant exposing my darkest truths. The next morning, I found a local victim counselling group. It felt terrifying yet necessary—it was my last desperate attempt to halt the course of my life, before all hope slipped away from me.

From Betrayal to Self-Realisation

Walking into that first counselling session, my heart pounded, my palms slick with sweat. The room was filled with faces etched in pain, each a mirror of my own suffering. As I sat among them, my throat tightened, my voice trapped beneath the weight of unspoken trauma. Now, faced with the prospect of laying it bare before strangers, I felt exposed and raw, like my wounds had been torn open once again.

Despite the struggle, I shared fragments of my story. Each word was like a slow exhale, a cautious release of the weight pressing down on me for so long. The room's empathy was palpable. For the first time in what felt like forever, I didn't feel utterly alone. The air thickened with unspoken solidarity.

But this glimmer of hope was short-lived. By the second session, the fragile security I had begun to build crumbled beneath the weight of a new, devastating betrayal. The very place I had sought refuge in became another site of trauma, plunging me back into the darkness I had so desperately fought to escape.

The group sessions mixed shared agony with tentative hope, voices filled with sorrow, echoing my own pain. I felt a strange connection to the others, as if, through their suffering, I could begin to piece together my shattered self. One counsellor, a man in his late forties, stood out. His calm demeanour and authoritative presence promised safety. His voice was soft, gentle, a balm for the raw wounds I exposed in those sessions. He had a way of looking at me like he understood, like he truly wanted to help. I trusted him. We all did. In a world that had betrayed me so many times, he felt like a light guiding me through my pain.

After one particularly gruelling session, where I had shared more than usual about Peter's addiction and the betrayals I had endured, the counsellor offered to drive me home. It was raining heavily, and though I hesitated, his gentle smile reassured me. I wanted to believe that kindness could exist without ulterior motives, that someone in this broken world could care without wanting something in return.

The drive was unnervingly quiet, the rain pounding against the windows, drowning out the rising discomfort in my knotted stomach. I tried to push aside my unease, reminding myself he was a counsellor—someone trained to help.

When we arrived at my apartment, I thanked him and prepared to leave, but he insisted on coming inside for a coffee. Just to check on me, he said. Torn between suspicion and the desire not to appear rude, I relented. After all, he was supposed to be someone I could trust.

But the moment he stepped inside, something shifted. My apartment, once my only sanctuary, felt suddenly smaller, darker, as though the walls were closing in. He sat at the kitchen table, and what began as casual conversation quickly turned uncomfortable. His comments about my appearance made my skin crawl, but I was too stunned to react. Then, with an audacity that left me speechless, he confessed his attraction to me and suggested I leave Peter for him. He seemed certain that he was the man to protect me.

As I listened to his words, I looked at him in disbelief and disgust. My mind began to race, I was quickly beginning to understand my discomfort in the car. I quickly replayed my interactions to see if I had led him on in any way. I couldn't understand why he singled me out. Many women at the sessions doted on him, why me? I felt hurt that this man, whom I had trusted with my deepest wounds, was now twisting them for his own desires. I declined, my voice barely a whisper, trying to explain that I wasn't in any position for a relationship—that I was broken, in crisis, seeking help, not this. I was still unsure how this had all transpired. But he was not in the mood to be rejected.

His face darkened, twisted with anger. Then, before I could even register what was happening, he lunged at me. The force of it knocked me to the floor, the breath sucked from my lungs as he pinned me beneath him. Panic surged; my mind raced for an escape. His eyes, once so compassionate, were now filled with rage and entitlement. I kicked, scratched, did everything I could to get free, but he was stronger.

And then I saw it—the kettle on the stove. Boiling water. Desperation fuelled my strength, and with one final push, I broke free, grabbing the kettle and holding it as a shield between us. My hands shook, but my voice came out steady, filled with fear-tinged resolve: "Leave. Or I swear…"

For a moment, he hesitated. Then, with a flicker of something—fear, perhaps—he left, disappearing into the rain as if he had never been there at all. I locked the door behind him, my whole body shaking as I collapsed onto the floor. Sobs tore through me. This man, whom I had thought was there to help, had violated my trust in the most horrifying way.

The next session loomed, and though everything inside me screamed not to go, I forced myself to attend. I was determined to confront him, to expose the predator hiding behind a mask of kindness. But when I arrived, he was gone. A new therapist led the session, offering no explanation for his absence. I sat there, numb, barely able to process the words spoken around me. As I sat there, my mind numbed by the weight of betrayal, something primal and fierce shifted within me—a voice that had been silenced for too long. It screamed at me that I had to get out – GET OUT NOW! I whispered, 'I must save myself.'

Without speaking, I unapologetically jumped up and ran out of the hall, like my life depended on it. I stumbled into the streets of New York. The heat, the noise, the chaos of the city—all of it crashed over me. Yet, through it all, there was a flicker of awareness. At that moment, I understood that no one could save me but myself. I wasn't just a victim—I was a fighter. And though I had been broken, something within me refused to die. That flicker of hope, that ember, would grow. It would ignite the fire that would lead me back to myself. This was my awakening to a new life.

Choosing Myself!

When I made the decision to leave New York for Texas, my life had been shattered by addiction, abuse, and betrayal. The years spent with Peter had broken me in ways I could never have imagined. I loved him fiercely, even when that love became a prison. But now, I was no longer bound by the chains of fear, abandonment and self-doubt.

It wasn't Peter I was truly afraid of losing—it was the story I had created for my life. The narrative that my worth was tied to saving him. It was time to write a new story, one where I no longer measured my value by someone else's chaos. Leaving was the hardest thing I had ever done, but staying meant continuing to sacrifice myself to a battle I could never win.

In Texas, I found the courage to confront my deepest fears that had held me hostage. For so long, I had been trapped in the belief that love meant enduring pain and that loyalty meant losing myself. I wasn't just walking away from Peter; I was walking toward myself—the real me, buried under years of trauma and survival.

I started working for a tech company, re-enrolled in school, and completed my degree in business. Later, I earned my master's in business. I left my life with Peter far behind, and apart from this writing, no one knew about my suffering. But here it is, so that you can witness my lack of shame or sadness.

The Unexpected Call

Months later, Peter reached out. He had finally committed to his recovery and asked for my forgiveness, and if I could meet with his therapist. I agreed because I wanted to support his recovery. I was proud of him. When I met the therapist, I didn't walk into that room to heal our relationship—I walked in to close the door on the life that had nearly destroyed me.

The therapist asked me to name the emotions I felt—anger, sadness, betrayal. But none of those captured what I truly felt. For the first time in years, I felt excitement—excitement for the life I was now free to live. I realised that Peter's pain was no longer mine to carry. His addiction, his suffering, his choices—they were not my burden.

When I said those words, the room fell silent. Peter, the therapist, even I was struck by the power in letting go. I wasn't angry anymore. I wasn't sad. I wasn't in love. I was free. And that freedom was something no one could ever take from me ever again.

The Phoenix Rising from the Ruins

The warmth of the Texas sun on my skin reminded me that I had survived the storm. And I hadn't just survived, I had risen from the ashes, stronger, wiser, and more determined than ever to live for myself.

I no longer saw my years of suffering as wasted. Those years had shaped me, teaching me the hardest lessons of my life. As I began volunteering, helping others still trapped in the darkness I had escaped, I realised that my journey had given me a gift—a gift of empathy, strength, and resilience.

And now, I want to share that gift as a motivational speaker, guiding others to find their own doors to a new future.

I now help people unlock their potential by finding their authentic selves by learning how to shift their identities.

To connect and receive my Newsletter please scan the QR code

ABOUT THE AUTHOR

CAMILLE WORDSWORTH

SCAN TO KNOW MORE

Camille understands the mental pain of waking up with dread, facing relentless pressure, and the anxiety of looming layoffs. With an MBA and over 20 years in finance, Camille was laid off multiple times, enduring the emotional toll of career transitions. Yet, she found these setbacks to be life's course corrections, not failures. Now a successful entrepreneur, happiness coach, and author of Forget the Corporate Bollocks! and A Life of Flow, Camille blends business insights with spiritual wisdom to help professionals in transition conquer fear and embrace change. Tune in to The Camille Show podcast on YouTube, Spotify and Rumble for free tools, strategies, and guidance to create a life you're thrilled to wake up to every morning.

CHAPTER 3

Singing without Chains,

Dancing with Freedom

CATHERINE PROCTOR

I was born on June 13, 1957. Until the age of 60, I believed I was born on a Friday— 'Whit' Friday, to be precise. On my 60th birthday, I decided to look this up to see if anything special was about to happen, you know, being born on Friday the 13th. To my shock and horror, I found out I was born on a Thursday. I wonder if that makes me a year younger.

I am the second eldest of five children. My dad died before I got the chance to meet him. All I knew was that he was a great swimmer, an alcoholic, and the reason my mum couldn't move to Australia when the government offered the £10 pom—he wouldn't go. He drowned in the River Liffey in Dublin after being at a funeral with his friends from the halfway house. They dared him to swim across the river while drunk, and he did. It was four days later before the authorities fished his body out of the river.

Life was difficult at home. Mum worked, leaving the older children to care for the younger ones, which was normal in those days. We always had lodgers in the house, as Mum hoped to open a B&B one day. The house was always chaotic; you never knew what lodger you would meet in the hallway. There were big navies farting in the bathroom, eating cabbage and bacon downstairs, which used to make me sick. One of them even asked us to play with him until the white stuff came out. FFS, I was only around 9 or 10 years old.

As I start to remember my own pain and childhood, being brought up in a loveless home, I try to recall a time when I felt loved or praised for something I had done. There was one occasion — I think I was five — I had chickenpox. My vest was stuck to my body. Mum gently dabbed every spot away from my vest and my vest away from my skin, being careful not to hurt me any more than I was already hurting. I remember she bathed me, wrapped me in a towel, and hugged me. I remember that feeling so well; I don't recall ever having it again.

To be honest, I do not remember any adults liking me. I was off school once for six weeks, and when I returned, everyone in the class thought I was a new girl. I was told by my teacher to stand on the table and recite my 8-times table since I had been away so long and must have learned something. I think I was 9. I stood on the table, and every time I got one wrong, the teacher hit me across the back of my skinny legs with my short dress and short socks. He would make me twirl around. We all know what was going on there. Such a cruel man. I met him years later and reminded him; he laughed.

By the time I was 13, I started playing truant; shortly after that I began drinking cider. It was disgusting, but I pushed through it for the buzz I got before it made me sick, and so the cycle began.

I would run away from home. Coming from a large single-parent family meant I could roam the streets as Mum was always busy, always under stress, and no doubt depressed. Mum and I never really got on; We fought and argued, and I would often get hit with whatever was close by. I was very defiant and just laughed, which only made things worse.

To be fair, my mum must have been extremely depressed; she had a hard life struggling with her kids on her own, working, and searching for love, which she never found.

By the time I was fifteen, I had managed to put myself into care. I loved this—living in a beautiful house in Didsbury, South Manchester, run by the Nuns. It was an all-girls home, each of us with our own set of mental health issues. We had our own bedroom, and it felt like a palace. I went to work and college. Things were looking good. The nuns gave us an allowance every month.

One of the girls, Maria, was Czech and a professional shoplifter. She had a club foot, so no one stopped her in the shops. We would pick what we wanted, and she would shoplift them for us, and we paid her. Maria was abandoned by her parents as a young child, and she was saving up to go back to the Czech Republic to find them.

Then there was Babs, who had been molested by both her father and brother and had a baby when she was just thirteen. I made a special friend at that home; her name was Christine. She was abandoned by her mum, along with her two sisters, and was found on a croft in a pram with only newspaper to cover them. Life was tough. Somehow, we all felt safe there, escaping our lives full of abuse, violence, dysfunctional homes, depression, neglect, and poverty.

I used to go out every weekend and lie to the nuns about my whereabouts. I would stay out all weekend, hanging around the late-night clubs in Moss Side, Manchester. I would sofa-surf, hoping to get a couple of hours of sleep before going back to that home. I was living a dangerous life, drinking, staying out, and mixing with strangers.

If I had been given more care, guidance, and love, then what happened next probably would not have occurred.

The Weight of Unsaid Goodbyes

I am leaving the care home I have come to love after living there for two years. I am taken to a foster home in Gorton, my care worker drives us there in perfect silence. When we arrived, my first thought was that the house does not smell clean—there were cats, and I'm not a fan. I cannot remember the lady or her name; she takes me to my room, which is not pleasant—nothing like the care home.

I go to the bathroom; there is a shower over the bath with a blue plastic shower curtain—the type that sticks to you when you're having a shower.

Every morning, I get ready for work in my room and leave the house for the day, often not returning until late. One of the girls I work with befriends me; she takes me to her home, which is beautiful. Her mum is a seamstress, and she makes me a pair of dusty pink trousers. They're bigger than I wanted, so she puts extra buttons in the waistband so I can adjust them.

Things are not going well at the foster home; the lady tells me I need to find somewhere else as I don't seem to be happy there. My social worker takes me to my mum, who has agreed to have me.

My Secret

One morning, I go to my mum's bedroom and tell her I am in pain, that I've been in pain all night, walking up and down the room. Mum jumps out of bed; I can see panic in her eyes, and she shouts, "This is it!" I look at her, but I'm in too much pain. Mum goes next door to ask the neighbour to help with my brothers and sisters; she also calls a taxi. It is September, and the sun is shining. We get into the taxi; I am in a daze. "Hurry up!" Mum keeps saying to the taxi driver; it's rush hour, and we're going to Withington Hospital. I can see my mum's face, white and strained. She puts her hand on my leg and says we will be there soon.

We arrive at the hospital, and everything is a blur. I can hear nurses calling, and I'm on a bed. I cannot see any faces.

I woke up in a hospital bed, alone in a room that felt both familiar and alien.

As I lay there, everything felt surreal, like a dream I couldn't quite grasp. Each time the door creaked open, my heart raced, not knowing if it would bring answers. I could feel a heaviness in the air, a tension that was almost tangible, but I couldn't understand why.

When the nurse finally entered, her footsteps echoed against the cold tile floor, She approached with a kind of urgency, her voice breaking through the haze of my thoughts. "I'm sorry," she said, I hear her words, but I don't understand.

"The baby didn't survive".

My mind struggled to comprehend what she said as the beeping machines continued their relentless rhythm, now a haunting backdrop to the shocking news I could barely process.

"What do you mean?" I am confused; had the baby been born? She explains that when I came to the hospital, it was time for the baby to be born, but it was too late to save her life. I am numb and in shock; I do not know what to say. She tells me the baby was a girl and asks if I would like to give her a name. I call her "Samantha." The nurse says she is sorry for me. I tell her I was going to have the baby adopted. There are no tears, just shock. The nurse says, "Oh, well, maybe it was for the best then." WTF!

I remember asking later that day where the baby was and whether there would be a funeral. I cannot get this exactly right—did I dream it or make the response up?

As the baby did not breathe, there would be no funeral, no burial. I am not sure if the next part is correct, but it is what I remember: "She told me that the body would be incinerated!"

I never checked what happened; I almost felt like I had no right. I asked the midwife who visited me about a death certificate. "Oh, you don't want to worry about that," she said. She said that it was over. "Pick yourself up and start over again."

There was no death certificate; she did not have a name. I secretly called her "Samantha". There would be no acknowledgment that she ever existed—a full-term baby born with her eyes closed.

You see, this was the reason I had to leave the care home. I never visited a doctor or went to an antenatal class; no one from social services came to see me. No one ever spoke about that incident. My trauma! We never discussed it again.

There was no one to help me with my grief.

Instead, I continued as if nothing had happened, nothing had changed in my body or my young life. My friend's mum knew that was why she put the extra buttons in the trousers; she never said a word. She used to cook nice food and sometimes would stroke my head.

Eventually, I got better and started working again. I was slim, so no one ever knew what had happened to me. I never cried; I just froze this memory in the pit of my stomach so deep I did not think it would ever rise again.

I just drank all the time. I would go out after work, drink, and listen to Marvin Gaye "What's Going On" album, in the deepest, darkest hole I had ever been in, drifting, hardened to anything that touched me—like a mechanical robot going on with my day-to-day life, always a mess, moving from one bad situation to another. I was 16 or 17 years of age.

Born asleep

Forty-two years later, I come across a headstone that simply says:

"She was born asleep."

This makes me cry and cry, and I am crying now. For the first time, I cried for you, Samantha. I suddenly understood you were born asleep. You had no one—a tiny baby who did not get to breathe, to look and see her mum's face. Who knows what the outcome would have been had you taken that first breath?

I used to visit the grave often, and still do when I am at the cemetery. I would say a prayer for Samantha, and for the first time, I acknowledge her existence.

I regret I didn't see you; I have no idea what your face looked like, but I am sure it was beautiful. I couldn't count your fingers, your toes, or smile with you. Our cheeks did not touch, nor did I feel your breath on my neck. I hope the angels have taken care of you. For the first time, I say

"RIP, my baby, who was born asleep".

I must stop writing now as I remember those days—the times when no one knew how to care. No one offered me anything. Just told me to get on with it. Get on with something so mammoth, something that until now, I never had the courage to talk about.

No one told me about antenatal clinics, or whether I even had a doctor. I just ignored what was happening, and so did everyone around me. Is it any wonder I was able to live two lives, always hiding from the truth, the reality, the hidden pain, masked by drinking alcohol and listening to my beautiful music?

I never had a role model—someone to show me right from wrong, someone I could trust, someone who made me feel safe. Someone who looked out for me, who made me feel loved and not worthless. I was left to roll around like tumbleweed, gathering more weeds until one day I found my own strength. This took many years and more traumas than I care to mention.

I know my mum did her best to care for me after the event, but how could she understand my pain when she couldn't truly understand her own? I thank her for what she did, for taking me to the hospital, and for looking after me when I got home. I am sure this was traumatic for her.

I am sorry to my girls for never telling you.

I have always believed this was something to be ashamed of—to hide away. When really, I was just another victim of circumstance.

Unable to cry for 42 years about one of the most traumatic happenings in my life. I have cried now.

After this, I started going out, hanging around in clubs and then to the all-night drinking places just outside Manchester, and here comes another...

The Cost of Keeping Quiet

On Saturdays, we used to go to a club in Manchester called The Explosion — and it truly was an explosion of music. Black music, soul music, songs that never hit the mainstream or played in popular nightclubs. Music has been my saviour over the years, and I'm not ashamed to say I'm a little biased about what I listen to. For me, it's always Black soul music.

The Explosion closed at 2 a.m. We are not going home. We jump in a taxi and head to the infamous Moss Side, a Manchester suburb known for late-night drinking.

Moss Side had its own vibe. During the day, it was a wonderful community of families, each going about their lives — a rich tapestry of culture and ethnicity. But at night, with all the city clubs closed, Moss Side came alive with blues bars that stayed open until six or seven in the morning, often inside private houses. These were the legendary shebeens.

As an outsider and still young, I found Moss Side a bit frightening, but that didn't stop me. The pull of the night, the danger, the music — it all gave me a sense of belonging. The infamous Reno Club transported me to another world. DJ Persian played records you never heard anywhere else; he's the one who introduced me to Marvin Gaye's *"What's Going On"*. That club was filled with danger for a young girl but also with excitement and intrigue.

It is 4 a.m., and Reno has just closed. I am in the café next door, grabbing my usual — a curry patty, a Moss Side (Caribbean) delicacy. I stuff it in my mouth, starving from being out all-night drinking. As soon as it has gone, I wish I'd bought two, but it's too late; the café is shut.

I can still hear the music from The Nile Club, a blues bar (a shebeen) above Reno. It is 5:00am, we wander along Princess Road, Then Mr. X comes along. I know him from the clubs and the streets; we occasionally have a bit of banter. I can tell you he was very handsome — short, mixed race, cool, and charismatic. He comes over to us.

"Hi girls, what are you doing out so late?" he asks, like the big bad wolf talking to Red Riding Hood. "Where are you going?" He speaks in his cheeky, nonchalant manner. I tell him, "Oh! We're just hanging out." He laughs, clearly a little high from the night's intake of weed and alcohol, as we all were, though I never smoked weed — just passively.

He invites us back to his place. His place! I can't believe it. Mr. Cool, the king of the street, is inviting us to his palace. But when we arrive, it is more like a shanty house, nothing like the palace I was expecting.

I'm feeling a strange vibe, standing at the front door. I thought he was cool, sophisticated? He quickly opens the door and pushes me inside, slamming it shut behind us and locking my friend out.

In those days, we were used to being knocked around, treated badly, without respect. We were young street girls who often had nowhere to stay, and we just accepted it. But this was different.

He has pushed me up the stairs. I am nervous, but laughing at the same time, still drunk, in shock at what just happened, we stop outside his door, I start crying, "let me go!" "I want to go." I try to move but he puts his arm out to stop me, he has pushed me into a room, a bedsit, I remember the musty smell, shirts hanging from the dado rail, and ironing board with the iron on top of it, by the one and only small window. I am now standing in the room cold shivering; I quickly sober up. I look at him.

He has taken his coat off, somehow, he no longer looks cool, and I am scared, really scared he looks strange and a bit twisted; he looks back at me. I beg him to let me go, he smirks "Take your clothes off" he says, he has a whip in his hand.

It was then I understood the saying "heart in your mouth".

I am sweating, I am cold; I know I am terrified. I still laughed with fear. But his face is not laughing, "I'm not joking" he tells me "Just do it." "Fucking do it" I beg him to let me go, I promise won't tell anyone, please just let me go, he has the whip flicking it at me, and now he has taken his clothes off standing in only his white pants, socks and a white vest, I remember that as I thought only very old men wore them, but hey that's what he was an older man dress up in young man's clothing,

My head is dizzy, I feel faint, he is jumping up and down with the whip, shouting! Skimming me with the whip slapping it on his hands, on the bed hitting me across my legs, when suddenly he jumps and pushes me onto the bed, he has gone wild, trying to get my clothes off, we are fighting, I am struggling to get away, he is stronger than me, still I fight, crying! Shouting! I am begging him to let me go, he will not stop. I am tired, hurt, fighting with every inch of my body to get away.

I am alone in a room with a stranger, my friend has gone, and he is about to rape me, I am weak from the struggle, there are other people in the house, they must hear the screams the shouts, but no one comes, each of them silent, behind their own door, maybe they are used to the sounds of screaming, of fear coming from the room.

He is jumping on the bed with the whip, hitting me trying to get my clothes off, my jeans are tight, he won't give up he is sweating, he puts his sweaty hand over my mouth/ face, I feel faint and sick by the smell and the taste, finally he gets the jeans off. I think I may have passed out with the exhaustion and sheer weight of the struggle; he finally gets what he wanted.

After that I try to move, he will not let me, he tells me I am his prisoner now, he puts his sweaty paws on my face, I am heaving, he smells of sweat, and I smell him. He finally sleeps, I try to move, he opens his eyes straight away, he tells me I am going nowhere, and forces his sticky self on me again, I lay still and hope it will soon be over, my strength to fight has gone.

I wonder what happened to my friend, did she come back for me? Did she run for the police? Or did she just roam until it was a safe time for her to go home. That is what we normally did, we would hang around the street, go back to someone's house who we knew, but one thing we never did was separate.

I did not shut my eyes, just lay there in that room, terrified what would happen next. The walls seem to be closed in making, the room seems even smaller, the smell was pungent, damp and sweaty. I can see the shirts hanging from the rail, the light coming in from the tiny window behind the cheap curtain.

I lie there wondering how I will get away, will he just let me go? He opens his eyes. It's late afternoon I think. He tells me I can go when he decides in the meantime, I am to work for him, I am his property now and I need to go out and earn money for him. He ties my hands together, there is a struggle but not like before, I am naked and very vulnerable. He hits me with the whip repeatedly. He punches me in my arms and then my body, I am alone crying in my heart.

Suddenly he gets up, irons one of the shirts, and dresses himself, and puts his bling on omg is he going out? Yes, he is!

He tells me to be ready for work when he gets back, he unties my hands, makes me stand up , hits me with the whip, and tells me to jump as he hits me, I cannot say No! I just do what he says, then he drops the whip, opens the door, and locks it behind him.

Am I alone? I didn't dare move, maybe I fell asleep, the door is locked, I am on the first floor and there is no way out. I got dressed, then I heard the door start to open, my mouth is dry, I am sweating, dizzy, but I am not letting him do that again.

I jump up and push the window open, as he comes in, he is laughing.

I have one foot on the windowsill, the iron is on, as he manages to grab me, I pick it up, I hold it to his face I tell him I will use it. My fear has been taken over by survival. I am on the first floor and must drop down onto a narrow wall then climb over a gate and run for my life. I just keep running. I had left my shoes there.

It's evening time. I thought it was Sunday, but it wasn't. It was Monday, I thought I was living with my mum, but I wasn't, I was living in a halfway house run by a catholic charity. When I got there my friend was sitting on the wall, she had just finished work and came to see if I was back. The nuns in the hostel told me I had to leave as I had stayed out and did not let them know where I was. I tried to explain, they did not listen, I just had to pack up my things and go.

I stayed at my friend's house that night. But one thing I know for sure is that I never told anyone what happened to me. I did not go to the police because I knew they would not believe me. A skinny white girl hanging around Moss Side at night? They would say I was asking for it.

I still went to Reno and saw him sometimes. He never came near me again. I heard there were other incidents, but I have no doubt he was a victim of his own circumstances.

Unbound: A Symphony of Freedom

My greatest aspiration has always been to become a journalist, a poet, a writer. When I was younger, I wanted to be the female version of Clive James—infused with his wit, fun, and charismatic presence—hosting TV shows like "A Postcard from...," wherever he roamed the world. He was enlightening and knowledgeable, capturing his audience through his television appearances, radio shows, and newspaper columns in The Observer. A truly talented man, without the usual educational background.

I bought a collection of his poetry, which remains an aspiration of mine: to write poetry that resonates and turns words into music.

Unfortunately, I did not achieve any of this in my early years. Instead, I opted for a laptop, a mobile phone, and a company car. I would walk into meetings feeling important, phone in hand, laptop case slung over my shoulder, dressed in a power suit with not a hair out of place. And after the meeting? Off to the wine bar to talk nonsense, showing off our latest padded shoulders and Prince of Wales check suits—pink shirts for the men. We thought we were cutting edge back then.

Looking back, I realize I could have pursued my dream of becoming a journalist. I won't fall into the trap of blaming every man and his dog for my choices. While I have endured immense trauma in my life, I have also been blessed with countless opportunities.

That said, what an amazing, eclectic, colourful, and wonderful life I have lived. From selling LPG—something I didn't even know existed until I applied for the job (and only because it came with a company car—I had sold my own to fund a rental property for my daughters and myself). I arrived an hour late for the interview in my red dress and black patent leather shoes, a look I got from Princess Diana. I met the Sales Director of Elf, and after two interviews he gave me the job.

I've worked and lived in Boston, setting up an online business for my dear friend, Mr Matthews. He was the first person who encouraged me to believe in myself. I first worked with him when he had a dating agency. Those days were hilarious, and I met some of the best people in my life, including my beautiful friend Jasmine, who remains in my life today.

I have sold property and lived in the USA, Spain, Turkey, Egypt, Hungary, and a host of other countries. I mean, what a life well-lived—a life of luck and adventure.

But my greatest achievement has been my ***'freedom-freedom'*** from the shackles of my traumas, from people who lack empathy, who don't have good hearts or kindness. And from those who couldn't wish themselves well, so they certainly could not wish me well.

It's the freedom to do what I want, when I want, and with whom I want.

What an achievement this is! I am so proud to say I've accomplished that.

We all have the power within ourselves to do the same.

Let's break that circle!

Who knows what's around the corner? Here I am today, privileged to be able to write my story—one book published and another on the way, alongside this amazing opportunity to be included in this book. We have all shared passionate, traumatic stories, which, for me, are only the tip of the iceberg.

You can read my story in full in my book, **'Twelve Words'** published by Bluemoose. It's available on Amazon, Waterstones, and through Bluemoose publishers.

I hope to be famous one day, and maybe I will be. I want to leave a legacy. I want my grandchildren to grow up with the highest aspirations, knowing they can achieve whatever they desire. I will be by their side, loving them and holding their hands for as long as I breathe.

I believe in a new generation of soft parenting, where mums, dads, and grandparents hold their children close, encourage them, protect them, and fill them with love and confidence—so they don't grow up writing the things we wrote about.

As I grow older, I understand the importance of "me" and my self-worth. I have come a long way from my dark days in Moss Side. I have learnt to love myself and accept who I am—warts and all.

With this confidence, I no longer worry about what others think or expect of me or what society perceives as normal. We are all our own normal.

I have set my own standards—a standard I live by. I do not judge, do not assume, and never knowingly hurt or upset anyone. I live with empathy and acceptance, recognizing that everyone has a story or struggle.

I will not be judged, nor will I care if you don't accept me. I am not ashamed anymore—just content. I am not afraid to stand up and shout that out loud. I don't care how you see me, or what you think of me, and I hope you feel the same way about yourself.

I will not live my life worrying about what others think. This makes me richer than any millionaire because I am rich with security, contentment, and love in my heart.

"What happened was not your fault!"

No woman should have to endure what I did and feel too ashamed to report it. For me, it was the time and era I lived in—a white woman in a Black community without a voice.

I hope this serves as more than just a story. If these words find a place in your heart, it may be because they speak to something you've experienced. If you see your reflection in these pages, then I want you to hear this clearly:

It was not your fault!

The weight of blame you carry, the heavy coat of shame—it does not belong on your shoulders. You were caught in a storm, not through choice. That is what storms do; they creep up on us, uninvited.

Talking about what happened may feel like reopening old wounds, but sometimes we must revisit those wounds to let the healing truly begin.

By sharing our stories, we discover we are not alone, and that our voices matter.

In time, you will learn to forgive yourself and move forward, knowing that life's experiences may shape you, but they do not define you. We are defined by our courage to speak and our willingness to embrace the truth.

To connect with Catherine & read her new Book scan the QR code

ABOUT THE AUTHOR

CATHERINE PROCTOR (CP)

SCAN TO KNOW MORE

Catherine Proctor (CP) is a storyteller, dreamer, and the co-author of Twelve Words, a powerful memoir that explores her journey through trauma, resilience, and healing. Writing has been her lifelong passion, rooted in childhood dreams of becoming a journalist and poet. CP's work aims to connect with others, reveal the strength within, and inspire the courage needed to break cycles of trauma.

Having lived in various countries, CP brings a unique perspective to her storytelling, enriched by a deep appreciation for diverse cultures. Her experiences have shaped a strong belief in the transformative power of sharing personal stories—narratives that foster understanding, drive change, and celebrate the resilience of the human spirit.

CP treasures her hard-won freedom and embraces life's adventures with gratitude and excitement. Through her writing, she seeks to empower others to pursue their dreams, embrace their true selves, and find healing in their own journeys.

Her memoir, Twelve Words, invites readers to join her on a path of resilience, self-discovery, and boundless possibility.

Read My Journey: *"Dive deeper into my story by reading Twelve Words', where I share my full journey of trauma and resilience. Discover how I turned pain into strength, and let my experiences inspire your own healing."*

Share Your Story: *Your voice matters! I invite you to share your experiences*

Reflect and Connect: *After reading this chapter, take a moment to reflect on your own story.*

Written by Catherine Proctor, Co-Author of 'Twelve Words'

CHAPTER 4

Echoes of Me:

Surviving Suicide, a Life-or-Death Helicopter Flight, and a Divine Encounter that Changed Everything

SARAH JOHNSON

Echoes of Self Hatred

I could feel the warmth of my phone as I pressed it against my right ear. It was the call I dreaded making. My body was flooded with fear—tingling surged through my legs and arms, and my stomach churned as I waited through the third ring. Then I heard a voice: "Hello? I'm here for you. What's going on?" The sound of tepid water filling the bathtub echoed behind me.

Earlier that morning, I had woken up gripped by absolute dread. It was a familiar sensation—every day had started this way lately. Self-hatred washed over me as I moved to place my feet on the cold hardwood floor. "Why do I have to do this again?" I thought as I walked to my closet, covering every inch of my body, hiding it from anyone who might see. I avoided the floor-to-ceiling, large black-framed IKEA mirror, unable to bear the thought of what might reflect back. "Everyone would be better off without me. I'm taking up space. I'm making everything worse," the thoughts echoed endlessly in my mind.

But today, those thoughts weren't just fleeting—they became plans. While some people daydream about their Friday night dates or upcoming vacations, I was daydreaming about my death.

At 32, with nearly 200 pounds weighing on my body and spirit, I stood in my closet, feeling the gentle pull of my 10-month-old baby girl, tugging at my oversized shirt for comfort, while my 2-year-old sang joyfully in the next room. But all I could think about was escaping — the pain, the constant pressure, the whispers in my mind. "Why can't you handle this? You're failing. You're nothing more than a fat, broken mom. No one wants to hear you; even your husband is pulling away."

I was drowning, overstimulated and overwhelmed, feeling like I would never measure up. I'd watch other mothers move through their days with ease, seeming to balance it all effortlessly, and wonder why I couldn't. My sense of self had vanished, and every attempt to reclaim it felt like another defeat. I used to be a career woman, thriving in philanthropy and social circles, yet here I was — struggling to recognize the person I'd become. Staring at my clothes, I began collecting the last outfit I would ever wear.

I had what many people would consider a dream life: a house with a roundabout driveway, some land surrounded by trees, and wonderful neighbors. A hard-working husband who took extra shifts to provide for us. Small children who knew nothing of the world's cruelties, squeezing my hand when we crossed the street because they saw me as their safe place. My fridge was never empty, and my utilities were always on.

So why did I want to die?

"I don't know why I'm calling." Yes, I do. I'm terrified. My eyes filled with tears as I checked the temperature of the water in the bathtub, ensuring it wouldn't be too cold and make me shiver before I died.

"Are you in a safe place?" The woman's voice on the other end of the line sounded like a caring aunt checking in.

"No," I replied, "I'm home alone, and I have a plan to kill myself. I need someone to know and call the police, so my husband and children don't have to be the ones to find me. I just want someone to care that I'm gone." The words flowed from my mouth like a bolt of lightning—effortlessly, as though I were saying hello to a stranger. It felt surreal. "Is this really my life? Am I really calling a suicide hotline?"

Just 30 minutes earlier, I had deliberately picked a fight with my husband, insisting he take the kids to the playground so I could have a break. I knew that if I were mean enough, he wouldn't want to be around me. That way, the last memory my toddler would have of me would be a smiling mom, waving from the driveway. I packed the diaper bag and snacks, ensuring they'd stay long enough for me to carry out my plan.

"How did I become this person? What had led me to this point?" So much had led me to this decision, but since you're reading this, you know there's a good ending. I'm still here. Unfortunately, this wasn't my rock bottom. There was more darkness I had to navigate before I'd find any light.

I spent what felt like an eternity on the phone with the guardian angel on the other end of the line. She kept me talking until my husband returned from the playground. She gently reminded me that I had value, even if I couldn't see it at that moment. The woman's soft voice broke through my train of thought "Your little girls will grow into women one day, perhaps facing their own struggles. If you follow through with your plan, they will be left with a lifetime of wondering why their mother didn't love them enough to stay."

Those words hit me like a punch to the stomach. I imagined my curly-haired baby meeting her first love, traveling to some distant place, and sending me a message saying she wished I were there to share it with her. I thought of my oldest daughter, standing on her wedding day, trying to get into her dress without her mother by her side. The weight of those images crushed me. And then, in the midst of that suffocating darkness, I heard the sound of the car pulling into the driveway.

"I'm not alone anymore," I told the anonymous voice. "I'll talk to my doctor. I'll get help." And with those words, the call ended, but my battle didn't.

In 2018, shortly after that day, I was diagnosed with postpartum depression and anxiety. Without proper guidance, the nurse practitioner prescribed me medication right away, and I drove straight to the pharmacy. What I didn't know then was that depression medication wasn't something you just stop taking. When the effects begin to fade, they simply raise the dosage. For two years, I drifted through life numb, as if a dentist had injected novocaine into my brain. Everything felt dull, distant, meaningless. But at least I wasn't suicidal anymore, right?

I wasn't really living, though. I was surviving.

In the Echoes of Self-Doubt

Determined to turn things around, articles about depression became lifelines, shared with my husband in hopes he'd understand how to offer support. Signing up for a half marathon seemed like a way forward, training through harsh weather as though punishment was deserved for even considering escape. "How dare you think something so terrible! Shame on you!" The relentless sting of shame followed, like a swarm of bees. Self-criticism became brutal, merciless, as if each step and struggle might somehow make up for the darkness within.

My mind had turned against me, and I had let it. I handed over the keys and settled into the passenger seat. From the outside, it looked like I was improving. I was laughing again, meeting friends for lunch at our favorite tapas spot in town. I was trying to repair the damage in my marriage, begging for forgiveness for the cruel things I had said and done. I knew the karmic trench I'd dug was deep, but I was determined to do whatever it took to save our connection.

The things we say in moments of pain and reaction often leave us with shattered pieces of something that was once beautiful. Our love and devotion had fractured under the weight of my words, but at the time, I didn't realize the root of it all: I didn't love myself. How could I really love him when I had no idea how to love myself?

It would take time. It would take patience. And it wasn't until March of 2020, when I contracted Long COVID and chose to stop taking all my medications, that I finally realized how far I had to fall before hitting rock bottom.

I'm grateful I hit bottom. It sounds strange, I know, but when you think about the vastness of that space—how dark and empty it is—there's nothing left to do but rise. When everything is stripped away, all that remains is the possibility of moving up and out. The following eight months were a whirlwind of physical symptoms: dizzy spells, migraines, breathing issues, and constant neuropathy—the pins-and-needles sensation that covered my entire body. Even simple things, like hugging my children or dialing a number on my phone, became excruciatingly painful.

By October, I noticed a tremor in my right thumb. It worsened with stress and—unsurprisingly—with coffee. So much coffee. As a mom of two little girls who seemed to avoid sleep like it was the devil, coffee had become my lifeline. But what began as a small tremor in my thumb soon spread to my hand and arm, until I could barely hold a fork to eat my usual garlic and spinach eggs in the morning. That's when I knew—I needed to see a neurologist.

Initial discussions with doctors included possibilities like Multiple Sclerosis, Parkinson's, and even brain tumors. Thankfully, after a contrast MRI and more blood tests than I care to remember, there were no signs of a tumor. But the mystery remained: Why was I experiencing this wide range of symptoms, and what had triggered it? Looking back now, it's entirely possible I didn't have Long COVID at all. I may have sent my entire nervous, cardiovascular, and endocrine systems into shock.

Depression medications can be a tool, yes—but informed consent is crucial. And I wasn't informed. I didn't know you couldn't just stop taking them. You have to taper off under the guidance of a trained professional. But I blindly trusted my doctors to lead me, unaware of how vital that trust would become until the morning of January 19, 2021.

Echoes of Desperation

My husband had just come home from a night shift at the hospital. I had gotten up early, like I did every morning now, with my new workout routine in place and a commitment to healthy eating. I wanted to be the best version of myself, even though the symptoms made it hard to dress or carry my daughter to her playdate. Still, I couldn't bring myself to look in the floor-to-ceiling mirror in my bedroom. By then, I had lost 20 pounds, but there was always more to lose. I think most women can relate—no matter how much you achieve, it never seems like enough to celebrate.

I walked down into our living room, where we had gathered weights and equipment to work out at home, since lockdowns and gym closures were still in effect. Our girls would sometimes crawl around our legs or mimic our movements during the workouts, but it had become a way for my husband and me to reconnect, to rebuild our marriage together. About ten minutes into the workout video, the room started spinning. I immediately dropped to all fours, knowing that if I passed out—something that had been happening a lot lately—I wouldn't hit my head.

With the room still whirling around me, my husband told me to lie on my back and take deep breaths. But when my daughter leaned over to "give mama a hug," I realized I couldn't move my right arm. My brain was sending the command, but my arm wouldn't respond. I couldn't reach across to touch her back, to play with her soft blonde ringlets. Panic set in as I looked up at my husband and screamed, "I can't feel the right side of my body!"

He dropped to his knees, taking my vitals. Everything after that became a blur of frantic action. We had taught our five-year-old what to do in an emergency: grab her little sister, now three, and run to the neighbor's house to call 911. My husband put that plan into action, and as my daughters sprinted down our stone driveway, my oldest yelled to the neighbor, "Daddy's taking Mommy to the hospital!"

Stumbling into the passenger seat with my husband by my side, I felt a strange sensation on the left side of my body as I tried to buckle in. A few minutes down the road, I turned to him, my voice trembling, "I'm about to lose all sensation on the left side too. Please tell them. Please tell them." I wanted to say, "Please tell the girls I love them." I had no idea what was coming next, but I couldn't bear the thought of leaving this earth without knowing they had heard those words. I had fought so hard to claw my way out of that dark place two years ago. I wasn't ready to leave—not yet.

Silent Screams in the ER

Thankfully, we lived just seven minutes from the local hospital—though it's only four when your wife is in the passenger seat with a medical emergency. As we pulled up to the entrance, the staff were already waiting with a wheelchair. My husband had called ahead, using his connections at the hospital to ensure the right people were prepared. To this day, I'm deeply grateful for the people who have crossed my path, especially those medical professionals who were ready to jump into action to save my life.

I wept, choking on guttural sobs, as the security officer lifted me from the car into the wheelchair. They whisked me through double doors and placed me on a gurney behind those thin, ugly blue curtains that provide no real privacy. My husband explained my symptoms and recounted what had happened, while his colleague listened intently and ordered an immediate CT scan. Most signs pointed to a stroke.

An active 34-year-old woman having a stroke isn't unheard of, but it's far from common. The CT results came back unclear. They couldn't locate the clot, but they also didn't have the necessary equipment to fully understand what was happening. And because it was Martin Luther King Jr. Day, the staff neurologist was off duty, leaving no one available to run the appropriate tests.

Now, I was faced with two options. The first was to wait—keep me comfortable, run more tests, and hope for answers. The second was more drastic: they could send me in a medical helicopter to a larger hospital further south, where top-notch neurology specialists would be ready to take over.

It's important to pause here and say that throughout this entire ordeal, my mind was racing at its usual pace. I was fully aware of everything happening around me. I heard the steady beeping of the machines I was hooked up to, saw nurses coming and going, and watched doctors speaking with my husband. I could see the worry in his eyes when they told him they couldn't find what was wrong. I could smell the sharp scent of disinfectant, freshly used to clean the room after the last patient had left. I could taste the bitterness of the medicines coursing through my system, as if they had been poured directly onto my taste buds.

By this point, I was failing every motor skills test. I couldn't push my feet against the doctor's hand, no matter how hard I begged and pleaded with my brain. I couldn't form words, only half-mumbled syllables and sounds. My husband was now making calls to those closest to me, uncertain of what might happen next. I will never forget the sound of my mother on the other end of the phone—a mix of raw fear and unwavering determination that nothing would happen to me. She and my dad love me, and they were praying for me.

I was trapped inside my own body, unable to move or speak. I had no way of telling anyone that I was still alive inside—that my mind was racing, desperate to act. It felt like I was already sealed inside a coffin, buried, with no one able to hear me banging on the lid to be let out. I was screaming in terror, but no sound came. In that moment, I realized that our souls and our bodies are separate things—something that would become important later in the story.

As they placed thick red straps across my body and tucked blankets around me, fear swallowed me whole. I didn't know what to do or how to cope with the sheer panic rising inside me. My husband grabbed my hand as they wheeled me toward the blue-and-white medical helicopter, its blades already whirring. A single tear slid down my cheek as he kissed me goodbye and let go of my hand. I couldn't say "I love you." I couldn't turn my head or even nod. All I could do was watch, helpless, as the nurse and the pilot lifted me into the helicopter cabin and locked the gurney into place.

They slipped headphones over my ears, and one of them tapped my shoulder, trying to reassure me that everything would be okay. But tears streamed down my face like a spring creek fed by melting snow. I didn't want this. I wanted to go home. I wanted to speak, to make it all stop. And then, suddenly, everything went black.

I lost consciousness and woke up as the helicopter touched down on the roof of a larger hospital, better equipped to help. I was rushed into the emergency room, surrounded by doctors, specialists, students, and onlookers. My only advocate in that crowded room was the helicopter pilot. I listened as he relayed my medical information, but I could tell he was missing key details. "Wait! Go back! You forgot to mention that… No, that's not right! Tell them this instead!" I was screaming inside my head, but no one could hear me.

I'm so grateful to the helicopter team for their care, and it wasn't his fault. But they didn't have the full picture—there was so much more they needed to know. I was utterly isolated, trapped in a body that couldn't move, while all those eyes looked down at me in confusion and concern. Then everything went black again.

Whispering Echoes from Beyond

In what felt like slipping from this world, a near-death experience, — a "being of light," radiated calm as if he had waited just for me. Every fear, every weight lifted as he spoke, revealing truths I had forgotten but somehow always known. "There's nothing to fear," they assured me gently. "You are safe; your purpose is greater than you realize." The peace I felt was profound, a deep, soul-stirring calm, like returning to a place I'd known before yet couldn't quite recall. "Welcome home," they whispered. "I'm so glad you're here."

When I asked who they were, their response was simple yet profound: "pure consciousness, the presence of God in you." They spoke of why souls choose to come to Earth, why we willingly step into lives filled with suffering. An ache began to fill the air, a sadness they carried for humanity's disconnection, knowing we feel so separated from one another, despite being one — bound by shared struggles and common pain. They urged that in reaching out to help one another, we could alchemize that pain, transforming it into strength, resilience, and an inner power beyond measure.

Despite the hardships I endured and the dark moments, when ending it all felt like the only escape, my purpose was revealed to me. "And now," God said gently, "the choice is yours: to return... or not." An overwhelming sense of honor filled me, knowing my path was one of service — to guide others back to their true selves, to the soul, the essence, the very core of who they are.

During this time, I came to realize we are far more than our physical bodies. Our souls hold the key to true joy and fulfillment. Yet, caught in the relentless rhythm of daily life, we lose touch with the innocent, playful parts of ourselves—the parts our souls still remember vividly. That childlike wonder, those boundless dreams, slowly fade as the weight of adult responsibilities takes over.

Ultimately, I chose to return, knowing my purpose was not yet fulfilled.

The Quiet Echo of a Distant Red Button

When I woke, the room was empty, and I was still trapped in my unresponsive body. I could see the small call button just lying there, inches from my fingers, but I couldn't reach it. I needed help. I needed someone, anyone, to rescue me. My husband had driven the two hours to get to me as fast as he could, with our little girls in tow. He had dropped them off at their grandparents' house and parked in the hospital lot. But they wouldn't let him inside.

Because of COVID-19 restrictions, he wasn't allowed in. He wasn't considered a patient. After working an overnight shift and managing my medical emergency, he had no choice but to take a nap in the car, completely shut out from what was happening. Desperate, he called the hospital, begging to speak with the emergency room staff. His voice was full of exhaustion and fear as he pleaded to be let in, or at least speak to my physician. They refused. They told him he would only get a call when they were ready to discharge me.

It was starting to feel like I was trapped in a suspense novel, where each page held more uncertainty, and I had no way of knowing what would happen next. I caught the eye of an emergency room assistant as she came to check on me. She saw the desperation in my eyes and seemed to understand that I needed help. A few minutes later, two men entered the room, their voices hurried and impatient. They told me I was suffering from anxiety, that I needed to reduce the stress in my life. Without running any tests or consulting my medical history, they decided to give me something to help me sleep, explaining that they needed my bed for a COVID patient.

I drifted into a medicated sleep, only to wake to an orderly shaking me. My vitals were good, he said, so I was being discharged. A doctor came in briefly, pointing to a stack of paperwork placed beside me in the wheelchair they had moved me to. Not a single test had been run at this top-notch hospital. No one had called my neurologist, the one I had been working with for months. No one had even contacted my husband to discuss the next steps.

I was essentially ejected from the medical facility, handed a few sheets of white copy paper, and given sympathetic glances from nurses who couldn't help me. The only positive thing I left the hospital with was a sacred memory of my encounter with God—a reminder that even in my darkest moments, I was met with a presence beyond understanding, a truth I will never forget.

Thirteen hours after my initial collapse, I was finally able to move my fingers and toes during the two-hour car ride home. Slowly, I regained the ability to turn my head from side to side, and I could just barely mumble one-word answers—"yes" or "no." I was starting to come back to my body.

Echoes of Ancient Wisdom

Bewildered and devastated by the day's events, I was gently helped into bed by my husband, with my girls snuggled up beside me. Over the next few days, my motor functions slowly returned, bringing with them a fragile hope.

When I visited my neurologist, he shook his head with a somber expression. "To truly understand what happened, we'd need another collapse episode to get a proper diagnosis and treatment plan." His words hit me like a brick. "Wait for another collapse?" I replied. "There has to be something we can do. I can't just... wait."

I couldn't let my five-year-old bear the weight of saving her stay-at-home mom, hoping her dad would be around if I collapsed again. I wasn't going to be a victim of my circumstances. There had to be something — anything.

Determined to find a solution, I turned to my community and began asking questions, refusing to give up. That's when I found an energy healer. Just six days after my collapse, I was lying on a table in his office, breathing deeply and slowly. He did what he does best, allowing whatever needed to happen, happen. Forty-five minutes later, every single symptom I had battled for the past ten months, was gone.

I sat up from the table, dazed and unsure of what had just taken place, but knowing in my heart that my life would never be the same. I felt God's presence once again, reminding me of the peace I find when I trust in my intuition and inner power.

I could now walk without pain rippling through my nerves from the neuropathy. I could hold my fork without the tremor that had haunted my every movement. I could finally sleep without the suffocating fear of being trapped in my body again. In the weeks and months that followed, I began to turn my life around in ways I never thought possible.

Echoes from the Wings of the Phoenix

Change is the one constant in life; it's the only certainty we can rely on. We are meant to evolve, to grow, to learn from every new experience and person who crosses our path. It's a comforting thought. Finding my voice has been one of the greatest gifts, especially since it was absent when I needed it most. Now, I stand as my own advocate. No one knows me better than I know myself, and this deep self-understanding is vital.

Years of overgiving, undervaluing, and sacrificing my own needs had left me depleted, with self-respect slipping away. As powerful lessons on trauma and its grip over my life emerged, I began to find peace in my journey back to myself.

I knew I could no longer play roles that stifled the person I was becoming.

After twenty years, my marriage came to an end. But I am grateful to say that we remain great friends, and we get along better now than ever before. Our children have two devoted co-parents, determined to provide them with love, stability, and adventure as they grow.

I have now lost over 50 pounds and established healthier routines that nourish my physical, mental, emotional, and spiritual needs. Every day, I feel more like my authentic self. My daily gratitude practice has become a cornerstone of my life, reminding me to honor my presence on this beautiful planet. I refuse to take it for granted ever again.

With my health restored, I began embracing the wisdom God shared with me. I learned to set boundaries, spoke kindly to myself in the mirror, and listened intently to the signals within. Gradually, I united body and soul, allowing both to guide me through each day.

Since this experience, my psychic and intuitive abilities have become far more prominent, offering a deeper level of insight and clarity than ever before. Though these gifts had always been with me, they now feel refined and purposeful.

Today, I use these abilities in my coaching sessions and course programs to serve others, helping them reconnect with the core of who they are. With each encounter, I guide clients back to their own inner wisdom, illuminating paths they may have lost sight of and empowering them to trust in their journey toward purpose and fulfillment.

Echoes of Love

I am just one voice in the world, yet every voice matters. If our stories and words reach even one person, they spark change, empowering that person to uplift someone else in turn. This ripple of connection is how we change the world, piece by piece. I believe that God calls each of us to work with love, and I am reminded daily that embodying love is the foundation of everything I do.

Living with love means showing up authentically, with vulnerability, and inviting others to do the same. I love connecting deeply, hearing others' stories, and offering compassion for the lessons they are navigating.

As a mother, I strive to show my two beautiful children what it means to turn life's challenges into personal power. Walking beside them on their journeys, I am honored to witness their growth and expansion every day. My greatest wish is for their future to be filled with possibility, and I am dedicated to providing them with the tools, support, and opportunities for self-discovery they need to thrive—both with my guidance and as they forge their own paths.

Through my work, I am bringing my message to the world — speaking on any stage that welcomes me, inspiring others to reconnect with their true selves and embrace living their life's purpose, with the sound of my heart, with Echoes of Me.

To connect with Sarah:

ABOUT THE AUTHOR

SARAH

SCAN TO KNOW MORE

Today, I have a thriving life coaching business, where I use my unique psychic abilities to tailor each session to the present moment, guiding clients as they navigate their own unique journeys. Living my life's purpose is an incredible feeling, and I wake up each day energized to begin. I'm constantly creating new materials that I believe will benefit many — responding to the unspoken requests of the souls I serve.

Each time we think we know ourselves, life has a way of humbling us, inviting us inward to reconnect with our true essence. Ask yourself: What are the values that genuinely define me? Which beliefs no longer serve my growth? Step forward with a commitment to rediscover the real you — the you who refuses to settle for anything less than a life aligned with your deepest truth.

If my story has resonated with you and touched something deep within, perhaps it's your own soul's gentle call for change—for a deeper connection to your true self. Imagine a life where you feel aligned, empowered, and truly seen, where each step forward is a return to the essence of who you are. I invite you to take that first step with me, to embark on your own journey of healing and self-discovery. Together, we can uncover the strength within you, reconnect with your true purpose, and create a life that reflects your deepest values. Let's walk this path of transformation, where you are supported, understood, and empowered to rise. When you're ready to answer that call, reach out—I would be honored to guide you on this beautiful journey.

START OVER VOL 1

CHAPTER

5

Broken bones, Unbroken Spirit:

Reclaiming My Power Back from Codependency and Abuse

STINA HELENEFORS

"And, when you want something, all the universe conspires in helping you to achieve it."

— Paulo Coelho

Never regret anything you ever choose to do in your life.

But what if you find yourself in a situation that is diminishing your own purpose and existence? Did I regret the journey that led me to that realization or not? I still ask myself that question.

The bustling terminal blurred, the noise fading into the background as my mind raced. A child's laughter broke through the fog of doubt, clear and bright. I watched her skip around, so fearless and free. "Kids don't overthink", I thought with a pang of envy. They just act.

But as I stared down the path ahead, I couldn't tell if I was running toward something or away from it.

People hurried past—families with tear-streaked faces, couples with warm embraces, solo travelers with unreadable expressions. Loneliness wrapped itself around me, sharp and cold. The familiar scent of coffee lingered, comforting for a moment, before being swallowed by the harsh, metallic smell of jet fuel. The contrast was jarring—just like my emotions, a whirlwind of confusion and doubt. The airport around me buzzed with chaos—footsteps echoing, loudspeakers crackling, conversations weaving together into a deafening hum. It felt like the world was spinning too fast, and I was stuck, frozen in place.

Is this really what I want? The thought echoed in my head as I stared at the blinking gate number ahead. It wasn't just a gate; it was a threshold, a leap I wasn't sure I had the courage to take. My heart pounded, uncertainty pressing in as each second ticked away.

As I moved toward the gate, my phone buzzed. It was a message from my best friend, Anna: "Are you sure about this? Call me before you board." Her words tugged at the part of me that wanted to run back, to cling to the safety of what I knew. But with trembling hands, I silenced my phone and stuffed it into my bag. I've made my choice, I told myself, the words heavy and bitter. This was the point where doubt met truth, where I would either stand firm or crumble under the weight of my decision. There was no turning back now.

As the plane lifted off, it hit me—I wasn't just leaving a life behind, I was diving headfirst into the unknown.

"Life is about choices, sweetie. Sometimes they lead to beautiful places, sometimes they teach hard lessons. But you have to make the decisions with your whole heart." My mothers words wrapped around me like a hug. Those words used to calm me, but now they felt like chains, holding me to a past I was desperately trying to leave behind. I'd just hugged her goodbye, the warmth of her arms still clinging to me, and as I remembered that farewell, fresh tears welled up. Part of me wanted to stay, to hold on forever, but I knew I couldn't.

At nearly eighteen, I had chosen to leave it all behind. The routines of the small town I once clung to now suffocated me. I craved freedom, a fresh start. But my heart fluttered uneasily—what if I was wrong? What if this adventure wasn't the escape I'd dreamed of?

My relationship with my mother has always been one of deep connection. She shaped me, her values becoming the foundation of who I was. But as I grew, I realized I couldn't embrace all of her beliefs. Her insistence on "doing things the right way" often clashed with my need to break free, to forge my own path. I'd learned to balance her wisdom with my own evolving views. "Mother knows best" would ring in my ears.

My new life would be far from the dreams and expectations I had built up and the reality of a life filled with darkness, abuse and codependency would hit me harder than I could have imagined. There was something about that pull, that tug-of-war between attention and distance, that fascinated me. But it was the one thing that would diminish my own identity.

Lost in His Lies: The weight of his manipulation

It wasn't the thunderous arguments that broke me—it was the quiet moments, the chilling calm before each storm, when his smile felt like a weapon and my love became my prison. From the moment I stepped into his world, the dream I once cherished began to unravel, each layer revealing the painful reality hidden behind the illusion of love.

From the very first moment, the dream I cherished so deeply began to fracture. At first, I was swept away by the excitement, blinded by the glow of a new relationship and the thrill of only seeing the best. But after a few months, as I became emotionally entwined, the reality set in—everything shifted, and the dream I once had was no longer the same. At first, it was subtle—the way his eyes lingered on me, not with affection, but with something darker, something cold and calculating. At the same time his charisma drew me in like a moth to a flame. He could be charming, intoxicating even, when he wanted to be. He knew just what to say to make me feel special, to make me feel like I was the center of his universe. But underneath that allure, there was always a darkness—one that I ignored, convincing myself it was just passion or intensity.

He could be very convincing, but his smile no longer felt warm; it felt like a mask. The questions started off innocent enough. I had only gone to buy groceries, a simple trip that should've taken no more than an hour. When I got home, his eyes were on me the moment I stepped through the door. "Where were you?" he asked, his smile tight, forced. The question hung in the air, heavy with accusation.

I thought I could fix him, but it was clear—this wasn't about love. It was about control.

The red flags were glaring from the start, my intuition sensing them almost immediately. Beneath the charm, I noticed the cracks—the subtle sting of his words, the sudden flashes of temper over things I couldn't grasp. Yet, I dismissed it all, telling myself it was simply part of his fiery passion, part of the allure that made him so captivating. Deep down, I wonder if I was drawn to the chaos, because it echoed the turmoil I hadn't yet resolved within myself. His affection filled that void for a time. But the highs didn't last, and the lows were devastating. I told myself that the good moments outweighed the bad, that he was just misunderstood, that if I tried harder, loved him more, things would change.

His personality, which had once made me feel safe, now made my skin crawl. I tried to brush it off, to tell myself I was overreacting, but the pit in my stomach only grew with each passing day. I felt like I was constantly walking on eggshells, every move I made scrutinized, every word I said questioned. It was like walking a tightrope, the ground always shifting beneath me, and I never knew when I would fall. Every day felt like a test I couldn't pass, and the life I had imagined—the love, the adventure—was nowhere to be found. I no longer recognized the person standing beside me, or worse, the person I had become.

I was living in hope.

The cycle felt endless, a cruel dance between hope and despair. On the good days, he would not apologize, but his voice was soft and filled with promises I desperately wanted to believe. He would tell me he loved me, that he would stop drinking and stop using drugs, that he would be the man I deserved. And for a moment, I'd let myself believe it, clinging to the memory of the man I once adored, the man who had filled my head with dreams of a life we could build together. But the good days never lasted.

I had spent years letting his words define me, believing that I needed him, that I was lucky to have someone who cared so deeply, even if his love came with a price. His validation was like a drug, and I was addicted to the fleeting moments when he made me feel like I was everything. I stayed because I didn't believe I could find anything better. I stayed because the fear of the unknown was paralyzing. I stayed because somewhere, buried beneath layers of self-doubt, a small voice told me this was all I was worth. That voice had grown louder over time, drowning out any whisper of hope I once had for something more.

His love, however twisted and painful, was still love, wasn't it? And I clung to that, convincing myself that I just needed to try harder, be better, be more for him. I whispered to myself, over and over, that if I could just be better—more patient, more understanding, more forgiving—then maybe, just maybe, he would change. But the truth I couldn't admit lingered just beneath the surface: no matter how much I gave, it was never going to be enough.

His manipulation had eroded my sense of self, making me feel small, invisible. He made me question my own identity, twisting every argument, every moment of doubt, until I couldn't tell what was real anymore. I was trapped—not just by him, but by my own fears, by the belief that this was all I was worth. Maybe I wasn't strong enough, or maybe I had convinced myself that this was what I deserved.

I wondered if this was my punishment for daring to dream of more, for believing in the possibility of happiness. The dream and expectations of love and respect filled my eyes with tears. I wanted to tell someone, to let the truth spill out, but the words stayed stuck in my throat.

"He didn't mean it," I whispered to myself. *"I just need to try harder".*

I felt so alone and like a little girl that just wanted love and safety. In those pitch-black, sleepless nights, when his cutting words still reverberated in my mind, and my chest tightened with the suffocating weight of his rage, it was my mother's voice that found me, like a soft lullaby drifting through the haze of time. My mother wasn't just my comfort—she was everything. She embodied strength, grace, and an unwavering belief in me. Every word she spoke felt like a guiding star, leading me through the darkest times. Her presence was a safe harbor, and her wisdom, though often gentle, had the power to shape my decisions and my worldview. I know she saw the red flags long before I did. I am certain of that.

"If you choose to stay, you must seek a proper education," she'd say, her tone both stern and loving. Those words became my lifeline, my savior, a thread of hope pulling me from the abyss. But as the story goes, it would take me many years before realizing the importance this would have in my life. I threw myself into my education because it was the one place where I felt like I had control, where I could prove to myself that I was worth something. But even as I achieved success, even as I earned recognition and respect in my studies, I couldn't shake the feeling of emptiness that haunted me when I went home.

Between the ages of 18 and 38, I found myself caught between two worlds: a life of successful studies, where I excelled and found moments of pride in what I could accomplish, and a toxic personal life that drained me of that very pride. My boyfriend's constant belittling chipped away at me, until every harsh word, every icy silence after our arguments, made me believe I was as small and worthless as he said I was. The contrast was great and I was living my boyfriend's lie everywhere, but at home, I was still that same girl, trapped in a relationship that was toxic to me, too afraid to leave and too broken to believe I deserved to. My self-esteem was like a fragile thread, always on the verge of snapping. I would hold on to that sliver of hope, even though deep down, I knew it was a lie.

Breaking Free: How I Left a Life That Wasn't Mine

"The most difficult thing is the decision to act, the rest is merely tenacity."

— Amelia Earhart

Fear gripped me, tight and unrelenting, squeezing the breath from my lungs. My heart raced, but I couldn't move. It was as if I had crossed some invisible line, one I didn't even realize was there, and now I was lost in a place where love had turned into something unrecognizable.

The crack of glass hitting the wall was like a gunshot in the suffocating silence. In that instant, the fantasy I'd clung to shattered alongside it. The broken shards mirrored my life—fragmented, dangerous, irreparable. The truth hit me harder than his words ever could: I wasn't here to save him. I was here to save myself.

The breaking point came one night, when I was in my 30s, when my boyfriend's drunken rage spiraled beyond anything I could bear. His anger was like a storm, wild and unpredictable, and I felt like a fragile ship caught in the middle of it, about to be destroyed. The sharp crack of the vodka bottle shattering against the wall pierced the silence, the pieces splintering across the floor like fragments of our broken love. The cold spray of alcohol slapped my face, its sting shocking me into a brutal, inescapable clarity, as if waking me from a nightmare I had been too terrified to leave. It was as though the icy sting of the alcohol was trying to wake me from a nightmare I had been living in for far too long. My hand, caught in the crossfire, throbbed with such a sharp pain that it stole my breath, the shock of it reverberating through my entire body.

I stared down at my injured hand, tears blurring my vision, and felt something inside me break. As the tears fell harder, something shifted. This—this violent, terrifying moment—was the wake-up call I had been too afraid to face. And in that moment, I knew—I had to escape. Not just from this immediate danger, but from the emotional and psychological wreckage I had been drowning in for far too long.

I drove myself to the hospital, my hand cradled against me, the city lights blurring through the tears streaming down my face. The physical pain from my hand was excruciating, but it was nothing compared to the emotional scars that throbbed beneath the surface. Each beat of my heart felt like a painful reminder of the life I was trapped in, a life that was slowly destroying me from the inside out.

Sitting in the cold, sterile hospital room, my hand now wrapped in a cast, I stared up at the fluorescent lights above me. Their harsh, artificial glow felt mocking, as if they were daring me to confront the reality I had been avoiding for so long. The silence in the room pressed down on me, and tears blurred my vision once again. The doctor's voice broke through the quiet, soft but probing. *"Did someone do this to you? Do you need to call someone? Family? Friends?"* His words pierced through the fog of my thoughts, but I could only shake my head, the weight of my silence pressing heavier than ever. *I have no one,* I thought, the realization crushing me. *He's made sure of that.* Over the years, he had isolated me so subtly, so effectively, that I hadn't even realized how alone I had become. No friends, no family—just him.

That night marked a shift within me. A small but determined part had awakened, refusing to be silenced anymore. As I returned from the hospital, I knew the confrontation was unavoidable. It would take another eight years of self-destruction and co-dependence before I could take the final step, even though my suitcase had waited by the door many times, like that night when he broke my hand.

I had to confront him, no matter how much it terrified me, no matter the pain it might bring. "We need to talk," I said, my voice trembling, but firm in a way it hadn't been in years. "About us.

He glanced at me, barely looking up from whatever was distracting him, annoyance flickering across his face like I was an inconvenience. "I deserve love and respect," I said, my voice breaking as tears streamed down my face, repeated as a shadow from my life's journey, but I didn't stop. I couldn't stop. "And it's not fair that you lie about your drinking and treat me like this."

His cold, dismissive stare sent a chill through me, but I stood my ground, trembling but resolute. For the first time in a long time, I realized that I wasn't the weak, broken woman he had made me believe I was. I was stronger than this. Stronger than him. And while the road ahead was terrifying, filled with unknowns, I knew I had to take it. I had to leave—before there was nothing left of me to save.

Before he could dismiss me with his usual indifference, I waited until he was intoxicated and tricked him into a fight. The tension between us escalated, simmering beneath the surface. When the moment felt right, I pulled out the divorce papers I had prepared. My hands trembled as I held them out to him, the weight of my decision pressing down on me like a final breath before the plunge. This was it—the moment I had been both terrified of and desperate for.

His reaction was swift. The anger flickered behind his eyes, igniting in a split second, and then his face twisted—an ugly, unfamiliar fury taking hold. I could almost hear it, like a hiss, the alcohol-fueled rage bubbling up inside him, ready to explode. But before he could lash out further, I pushed forward. The papers trembled in my hands as I watched him, daring him to cross the line he had danced on for so long. With sharp, deliberate strokes, he signed the papers. Each signature felt like a knife cutting through the ties that had bound us, severing the toxic connection that had suffocated me.

Leaving the toxic relationship at an age of 38, was just the first step. The twenty years of subtle manipulation, the constant erosion of my self-worth, had left deep scars. It wasn't just about walking away from him—it was about rebuilding the parts of myself that he had broken down, one cruel word, one dismissive glance at a time. Reclaiming my sense of self wasn't quick or easy. It was painful, messy, and required a level of introspection I had long avoided. I had to face the parts of myself that had been buried beneath years of shame and doubt, the pieces of me that had been hidden in the shadows of our relationship.

But I was determined, my life started on a complete transformation, but the wounds inside were challenging. I began piecing together the fragments of my life, learning to trust myself again. I started by setting small boundaries—things I had never allowed myself to do before. I began to protect myself, not just from him, but from anyone who threatened the fragile progress I was making. I reached out to old friends, the ones I had pushed away over the years at his insistence. Each conversation felt like a small victory, a step toward reclaiming the life I had lost. With each connection, each moment of vulnerability, I began to feel a sense of hope I hadn't felt in years.

There were days when the weight of the past felt too heavy, when the temptation to slip back into old patterns gnawed at me. But I fought it, knowing that every step forward, no matter how small, was a step away from the woman I had been—the woman who had believed she wasn't enough, who had settled for less than she deserved. And with each passing day, I began to see glimpses of the new, transformed future me, the person I was becoming - strong, capable, and free.

Through this painful but transformative process, I slowly began to develop something I had never truly known before—a sense of self-leadership. It wasn't an overnight change, but rather a quiet, persistent awakening that came after years of feeling powerless, of letting others dictate my worth, my choices, and the direction of my life. For so long, I had been caught in the current of someone else's desires, drifting along without questioning where it was taking me. But now, for the first time, I felt a pull to take control, to chart my own course with intention and clarity.

I realized just how long I had spent seeking validation from others—allowing their opinions, their approval, to define me. It was a common thread in my life, being victimized, instead of taking control of my life. The chains that held me were ones I had wrapped around myself, born from fear, insecurity, and doubt. Breaking free was the hardest thing I've ever done, but it was also the most necessary. It was the moment I realized that I was in control of my own story, that I had the power to shape my future. It was about finding the strength to believe in myself again, to trust that I was worthy of love—not the kind that suffocates, but the kind that lifts you up, that lets you breathe. And it was about learning that the most important love I could ever have was the love I gave to myself.

I had given away pieces of myself, bit by bit, believing that if I could just meet the expectations of others, I would finally be enough. But in doing so, I had lost sight of who I truly was. The realization stung, but it was also liberating. I could see clearly now that no one else had the right to determine my worth. That was something I needed to reclaim for myself, something I had to nurture from within.

In my early 40s it was time to take ownership of my life, to lead it with intention and not by the whims or demands of others. This wasn't just about healing from the wounds of the past—it was about rewriting my future, one where I was no longer a passenger but the driver. Reclaiming my story meant taking responsibility for my own well-being, making decisions that honored who I was and what I needed. It meant setting boundaries, saying no when something didn't serve me, and listening to that inner voice I had silenced for so long.

This was my life, my story, and for the first time in a long time, I was ready to lead it with purpose, strength, and unwavering clarity.

From Fragments to Fulfillment: A Journey of Rebuilding and Resilience

"When you're at peace with yourself and love yourself, it is virtually impossible to do things to yourself that are destructive."

— Wayne Dyer

Several years after the breakup and turning 40+ years, just when I thought I had regained control over my life, I encountered a new challenge: burnout. The relentless weight of emotional turmoil from my past relationship, compounded by the constant demands of my career, finally took its toll. Exhaustion crept in slowly, but before I knew it, I was completely overwhelmed—physically drained, mentally anxious, and emotionally lost.

I had thrown myself into my career, desperate to fill the gaping void left behind by the shattered pieces of myself. But the more I immersed myself in work, the more the long hours and endless pressure chipped away at my resolve. Another wake-up call.

One night I crashed and I hit rock bottom once more. I understood that the underlying thoughts I had were shadowing my wellbeing and I needed to fight back and work on the positivity of my soul. I found myself sitting in the bed with a large piece of paper and a rainbow of pens, determined to face the demons in my head. I began to write, my hand moving feverishly across the page. On one side, I scribbled the dark thoughts that had plagued me for years, the words that others had put into my mind—*I am weak. I am unworthy. I am lost.* On the other side, I wrote their opposites, words I desperately wanted to believe but couldn't quite yet—*I am strong. I am worthy. I am in control of my destiny.* These affirmations, though foreign at first, became my daily mantra. Every morning, I stood in front of the mirror, repeating them to myself, willing the words to sink in. At first, they felt like hollow promises, words without substance. But over time, they became my lifeline—, reminding me that change, though slow, was possible.

I found solace in understanding the science behind what I was doing. I devoured books on neuroscience, fascinated by the concept of neuroplasticity—the brain's incredible ability to rewire itself. The idea that I could literally reshape my thoughts, transform my mind's inner landscape, became a cornerstone of my healing. Each positive affirmation I repeated was a step toward reinforcing new neural pathways, a journey toward optimism and emotional recovery. Knowing that I could change not just my thoughts but the very way my brain processed those thoughts gave me hope. It was like learning to build myself anew from the inside out.

During the corona-year 2020, I made the life-changing decision to become a stress therapist. As I studied, I realized that my journey through trauma and burnout had given me profound insights into resilience, healing, and the power of sustainable self-leadership. This wasn't just an academic pursuit; it was deeply personal. Each lesson I learned in my training felt like another piece of the puzzle I was slowly piecing together, a reflection of the journey I had taken to heal myself.

My studies empowered me to heal from abusive relationships and burnout in a way I hadn't thought possible—by creating a balance that allowed me to thrive rather than merely survive. I began to envision a future where my story could inspire others, where the pain I had once tried to hide could become a tool for connection and empathy. I started to see my struggles not as a source of shame but as a badge of resilience, proof of the strength I had discovered in myself.

In January, 2021, I sat down and created my first vision board based on my true self, filling it with images and words that represented my new goals and dreams. This routine, this act of creating a visual representation of my future, became a trusted companion, guiding me back to a place of well-being and renewed energy whenever I faltered. I had successfully reprogrammed my brain.

The day I earned my qualification as a Stress Therapist, I felt something shift within me. I had risen from the ashes of chaos into a place of clarity and purpose. I was no longer defined by my past or the pain I had endured; I was defined by the choices I made moving forward. I had transformed, and I was determined to help others do the same. I had started to live a life that was aligned with my own values, a life that felt authentic to who I was. And in doing so, I had found fulfillment in ways I never could have imagined. My transformation wasn't just about leaving behind my past; it was about embracing a future full of possibilities.

By intentionally cultivating a more positive mindset, everything within me began to shift. The questions I started asking myself in moments of doubt, uncertainty, or even everyday situations became more than just reflections—they became the compass guiding me toward something greater. Slowly, they led me to a deeper sense of purpose, illuminating parts of myself I had long buried under layers of fear and self-doubt. Each question peeled back another layer, forcing me to confront my insecurities and replace them with a new, more empowering narrative.

My sense of self-worth, which had been chipped away by years of doubt and external validation, began to return in fragments.With each positive shift in my mindset, with every new question I dared to ask, I felt myself stepping more and more into the life I was meant to live—a life defined not by fear or limitations, but by purpose, self-love, and authenticity.

Years after my transformation began, I emerged not just stronger, but more self-assured than I ever thought possible. The broken, uncertain woman I once was had become a distant memory. I had reclaimed my life from the ashes of heartache and doubt. I had become the hero of my own story—one who was finally living a life true to herself.

With newfound strength and clarity, I embraced my role as a Resilience Strategist and Sustainable self-leadership consultant.

When I reflect on my journey, I often share my personal mantra: *"Life is a journey to find your true self. Once you've found it, hold it in your heart, and don't let go."* These words are a reminder that self-discovery is not a destination you arrive at once and for all. It's an ongoing process, a continuous unfolding of who you are and who you're meant to become. I realized that the road would never be entirely smooth; there would always be mountains to climb, storms to weather. But now, I no longer fear those challenges, instead, I lead my life with intention and purpose.

My transformation wasn't the result of one miraculous, life-changing moment. It was built on countless small decisions—to choose myself over fear, to choose love over doubt, and to choose authenticity over the pretense of pleasing others. Each step was hard-earned, but each one brought me closer to becoming the person I was always meant to be.

During this time in life, I developed the principles of Sustainable Self-Leadership and The Pillar Theory. It emphasized intentional living, self-responsibility, and the courage to grow. This philosophy not only guided me through my darkest times, but it became the foundation of my work, helping others find their own paths to clarity and renewal. It was about more than just overcoming; it was about thriving, about building a life that was both meaningful and lasting.

I started creating programs that promoted practices for increased employee and manager well-being. I knew from experience that when people feel supported, valued, and encouraged to care for their emotional health, they become more engaged, more productive, and more fulfilled. My work was about empowering people to live fully, to create space for themselves, and to thrive in ways they hadn't imagined possible. I reminded my clients—and myself—

that sustainable self-leadership isn't about perfection. *"It's about balance, about living with intention,"* I would say. *"It's about knowing when to push forward and when to rest, when to say yes and when to say no."*

And now, as I stand here, grounded in the woman I've become, I realize that every challenge, every moment of doubt, was a step toward my power. I no longer seek validation in others' expectations or in the roles I used to play. Instead, I own the narrative of my life with fierce grace. The burnout, the heartbreak, the struggles—they did not break me. They forged a version of myself that stands unshakable, ready to face the unknown with unrelenting strength. The road ahead is still full of choices, but now, I walk it knowing that the only permission I need is my own. And with that freedom, I choose to live boldly, to lead with resilience, and to embrace the limitless possibility of what's to come.

Key Lessons from my Story:

Reclaim your Power: True strength lies not just in walking away from toxic relationships, but in choosing yourself. By setting boundaries and prioritizing your well-being, you take control of your life. No relationship, no matter how deep or long-standing, is worth losing your identity.

Healing is a Journey, not a Destination: The path to healing is often long and winding. It's not about racing to the finish line but about taking consistent, intentional steps toward growth. Embrace the process, knowing that each small victory moves you closer to reclaiming your inner strength.

Your Inner voice shapes your Reality: The words you tell yourself hold immense power. By transforming your inner dialogue and nurturing a mindset of self-compassion, you rediscover the resilience that has always been within you. Speak to yourself with the same kindness and encouragement you would offer a loved one.

Turn Pain into Purpose: The challenges you face can become the greatest sources of strength and wisdom. By channeling your personal struggles into a greater purpose, you transform not only your own life but also the lives of those around you. Let your scars be a testament to your resilience.

Lead with Intention: Sustainable self-leadership is about making choices aligned with your values and goals. It's about balancing ambition with self-care, pushing forward when necessary, and knowing when to rest. Lead your life with clarity, knowing that each decision you make shapes the story you are writing.

To connect with Stina scan the QR code

ABOUT THE AUTHOR

STINA HELENEFORS

SCAN TO KNOW MORE

Stina Helenefors is a renowned author, Resilience Strategist and Leadership Consultant specializing in Sustainable Self-leadership and creator of the Pilar Theory. With a deep commitment to empowering professionals and organizations, Stina has dedicated her career to helping individuals lead meaningful, productive lives. Drawing from her extensive experience, she has pioneered tailored strategies that foster resilience, reduce stress, and cultivate positive, thriving environments.

Her programs not only focus on building resilience but also on enhancing overall well-being, creating a foundation for long-term success both personally and professionally.

For more information or to connect with Stina, follow her on social media and search "Stina Helenefors" to buy her books on Amazon:

Instagram: @sustainableselfleadership

Internet: www.sustainableselfleadership.com

CHAPTER

6

Ripping Up the Script:

My Fierce Rebellion to Find My Own Story

RADOMIRA SUNAVCOVA

Have you ever felt like you're living someone else's idea of what your life should be like?

I have. Not once, but several times, in fact.

There came a point in my life when it suddenly became clear that the path I'd walked wasn't one I'd chosen consciously. It was like realising that I'd been reading from a script – one that was written without me having any say in the matter. Drafted by circumstances, family dynamics, and the expectations of others.

What did I do? I woke up. Tore the pages out of the script and replaced them with my own.

Except – fast forward a few years and somehow, there I was again, speaking lines my heart wasn't feeling, striving for goals that I thought made sense, but weren't taking me towards the life I longed to live. Once again, I was accepting an external script as the only version of reality available to me. Once again, I ripped up the pages and tried again. And again.

Ultimately, as I've got older and found my confidence, I have embraced curiosity. I've learned to question the pages I've been presented with, and to keep on questioning them.

I've gradually understood that if I want to truly live, I need to keep starting over— not erasing the past but rewriting my story from a place of awareness, intention, and deep self-compassion.

This is my story. As I tell it, I invite you to think about your own.

Act One: Your Worth is in Your Appearance!

If you looked at the family photo album, you would probably think I was a happy child growing up in a stable family. In some senses, that's true. My parents were together, married, committed. We always had enough food on the table. My physical needs were met. However my earliest memories are of tension and arguments, of growing up with a pervasive sense of unease. I soothed myself with food to replace the emotional security which was missing. This became my first crisis.

You see, my parents' marriage began with a burden – and that burden was me. They married young, in their early twenties and not out of love but from a sense of duty, because they were expecting a baby – me. This foundation of obligation rather than genuine affection set the stage for a childhood fraught with conflict and resentment, between my parents with each other and my parents with me.

I once read that the more distressed the childhood, the less you remember of the details. Nature is very clever and wants us to protect from hurt and sadness. Accordingly, I am no longer surprised that I struggle to remember a single time when my parents held me and told me that they loved me.

The emotional neglect in my household extended beyond the volatile relationship between my parents to how they were with me. There was little attention given to my feelings, choices, or needs. Orders were given and I was expected to obey them. I learnt to be independent. Way too much for my parents' taste as I found later in life. But before you judge too harshly, let me be clear: I never suffered from hunger—in fact, quite the opposite. I always had clothes to wear and my room was filled with books and toys, but I felt an emptiness that could not be filled with things. There was no one to read me a story or ask me how I felt or what I was thinking. Although comfortable, my childhood lacked the essential nourishment of emotional connection. My mother, stressed and unhappy, often made me the focus of her frustrations. One day, for example, my brother and I were messing about in the kitchen, running around, chasing each other. Of course, something went wrong. I bumped into my mother while she was carrying a pot of boiling water and yes, the hot water spilled down my back. Instead of kind words, I received yelling and a smack right where the water had landed. This was a harsh lesson that in my house, there were no allowances for being a child, at least, not for me. Mistakes were not tolerated but would be met with shouting and criticism. This is part of my life script that I still find it hard to resist following. Even today, I struggle to tolerate mistakes, both in myself and in others. I am learning to reach for understanding, not anger.

My father wasn't ready for parental responsibility and often found his escape in bars. He worked hard to be able to support us, I know that, but he also played hard. He was rarely present with me and when he was it was only in superficial ways. He would give me toys, sweets, and trinkets, but never the attention or love I craved.

The closest thing we had to intimate time with my father was in his smoking room, where my brother and I were expected to be his quiet companions while he puffed away. He didn't want to be alone, but he didn't want to engage or interact, either. The room thick with poisonous smoke fumes, but the silence between us was also suffocating. In that smoke-filled room, I drew the conclusion that I was valued almost as an object, not for what I could contribute as a person. I wasn't asked how I was feeling or what I wanted to do. There was no interest in what happened at school. I learned that to be loved, I didn't need to be understood, I just needed to be *there*, silent, compliant, waiting for love to be given in the form of things, not words or care.

This wasn't a lesson I always internalised very easily. I could be opinionated, even rebellious, especially as a teenager and since my father's temper was also very short, frequently this resulted in yelling or the occasional slap. Yet again, I was being schooled to push my own opinions and expressions down to 'the basement' and to live life according to the expectations of others.

And now for the final ingredient – food, of which there was never any shortage, as I mentioned earlier. Looking back, I'd say that I wasn't the only person in my family who used food as a crutch or a substitute. In general, food was more than sustenance in my family. It was a tool for dealing with everything – for suppressing emotions, for celebrating achievements, for coping with stress. This pattern of emotional eating became ingrained in me from a young age. Whenever I felt sad, scared, or even happy, food was my go-to comfort. It became a way to numb pain I didn't know how to express or process. Over time, this led to unhealthy eating habits and a complicated relationship with my body. I learned to use food as a crutch, a way to fill the emptiness inside, but it never truly satisfied me.

Over the years, I became a strong girl with curves. This drew my father's attention and his negative judgement, expressed one day in words that would haunt me for years, words that cut deeper than any physical wound.

"No one will love you or want you if you look like that."

Laced with cold certainty, my father's words were a blow I never saw coming. I had no escape. I was exposed and vulnerable and something in me shifted, shattering. *I believed my father. I agreed with him.* His words didn't just hurt – they gouged a wound into my heart where shame and self-doubt would live for years to come. It was no longer just my father's voice I heard – it became my own. I looked at my body and saw it through his eyes, convinced I was unworthy, unlovable, unwanted because of how I looked. My reflection in the mirror became something to fear and despise. The weight I carried wasn't just on my body. It was in my soul. His words didn't just touch the surface; they rewrote the core of who I believed I was. I hated myself. I hated my body. And I set out on a mission to change it.

Act Two: Breaking the Vicious Cycle

When I first resolved to lose weight and get fit, I would have told you that this was my act of defiance, my rebellion to *tear up the script*. I think, though, you can see that even if some of the effects of my resolve were useful, the motivation was somewhat toxic. My drive sprang from my father's judgement about my body, which had become my own judgement against myself.

The consequence of my emotional eating had become impossible to ignore. Food, once my refuge from the chaos of my home, had turned into my enemy. However, in fighting that enemy, I also ended up fighting myself, driven by another unhelpful script, imposed on me from outside. The comments from friends and family only deepened my belief that my worth was tied to my looks. I didn't see my body as something to be loved or nurtured – it was a problem to be fixed. Desperate for acceptance and love, my life shifted until everything revolved around controlling how my body looked. I clung to rigid rules around food and exercise to keep me afloat. I wasn't motivated by desire to become healthy or build strength. This was about survival. I was consumed with the idea that through strict control, over every bite, every calorie burnt, I could sculpt myself into someone worthy of love.

Eventually, I decided to run away from it all. Still looking to start my perfectly scripted life, I came to London and embarked on my career as a Personal Trainer. It was a natural move since I spent the majority of my time either in the gym or active and exercising. From the outside, it looked like I had found my purpose, and I always enjoyed it. But I still had a way to go before I could free myself from the old scripts, before I could live, and work, in ways that were truly healthy and authentic.

Deep inside, I was still fighting the same battle. I believed I had to embody an image of fitness perfection to be taken seriously, to be respected, and most painfully, to be loved.

Looking closely, my life at this time was an excellent example of how "healthy" can become unhealthy. I now had the body I had spent so long dreaming about. I was finally "perfect" but I was dominated by anxiety about regaining weight, terrified of being out of control. So much so that I would avoid social occasions out of fear of being judged because I didn't want to eat or have a drink. I couldn't wait to be back at the gym at 6am on a Saturday morning. I quickly felt at home in London but although I had successfully escaped from a context where people constantly commented on my appearance, I had not escaped my attachment to that script. My programming sought out those conversations even when I thought I wanted to leave them behind. Somehow, I always ended up in a circle of people who were occupied with looks, including my partners. The unhealthy obsession about looks and thinness felt too familiar and, in a strange way, too comfortable. I didn't realize that my narrow focus on appearance had alienated me from the true essence of health—balance, well-being, and self-acceptance, not punishing but nourishing. Looking back I only can apologise to all the people and clients I came across then. Because there was only one way of being, of looking. I wish I could take the time back and say to all these women and men that it isn't true. You don't have to shrink to live, to be loved. I perpetuated their belief. I myself did not know better. And we went on.

To shake myself free from this version of my life-script, I took two different, painful wake-up calls. First, I lost my menstrual cycle, a problem which persisted for almost a whole year. When I looked for help, I was told that this was absolutely normal and could be controlled using birth control pills. I knew this wasn't the answer for me, so I started to do my own research. I reflected on my lifestyle and made a decision to change my diet and reduce my caffeine intake – which at the time was as much as eight cups a day. It was very difficult to overcome my fears about what would happen to my body if I let myself eat a bit more and exercise a little less. For others this was such a rational and appropriate step, but for me it was incredibly difficult.

Even so, I knew I had to do something. Our cycle is one of the major indicators of a woman's health! It took me 7 months to get my cycle back. This was the first step towards my freedom and it felt like a significant achievement. Slowly, I was reaching towards a different version of my story, one where my external looks were no longer the most important thing about me. I began to see that a healthy and fulfilled life can look different from what I had assumed or longed for, before this problem manifested.

The second wake-up call happened not in my adopted home of London, but while I was visiting my family back home.

My brother and his wife had a son and I wanted to spend as much time as possible with him. I was only supposed to be there for three days but this trip very suddenly turned into a stay of four months after I fell down on an icy path and tore my meniscus. I'd been having knee trouble for some time, linked to my levels of activity, but this was another level entirely. The fall resulted in the removal of my lateral meniscus, and I found myself bed-bound.

You can imagine the challenge this represented. I had tied my whole identity to movement and now, suddenly, I was confined to bed and facing the possibility that there were some forms of exercise I would never be able to do again.

At first, I was broken, depressed and anxious, haunted by the fear of gaining weight during recovery. This mindset was incredibly draining, both physically and mentally but gradually I found my way past it. Partly, this came about as I followed my surgeon's advice, but the key turning point was when I found the confidence to create my own, modified training routine. I progressed bit by bit and suddenly found I had bounced back. Yes, I had to accept that there are some things I could no longer do. I missed (and still miss) running so much but I swapped it for cycling and found new benefits from this new form of activity. If there is a will there is a way!

This difficult season became a time when the old stories loosened their grip. I became more open to alternatives, a lesson that significantly supported my psychological growth. However, I was not yet entirely free. Although my approach to wellbeing started to shift, my internal attitudes still needed to change. Some of the beliefs deeply rooted from my childhood persisted.

I was still chasing external validation and desperate for someone else who would tell me I was good enough, pretty enough, thin enough. Someone whose opinion I could use to shore up my shaky sense of self-worth. In this area of my life, I still needed to change the script.

Act Three: Relying on Somebody Else Won't Fix You

Act One of my story was about the scripts I received from my family-of-origin and how deeply the stories I was expected to conform to became internalised. In Act Two, through two experiences of ill health, one chronic and the other acute, I resolved to break free from the script of body perfection – and maybe I thought that the work was done. But another story was also at play, a story about the life a woman is supposed to have, and the age by which she should have it.

Now, in Act Three, I had to decide whether to cling to expectations or break free of them.

My last relationship fizzed like fireworks in the beginning. It was a room full of candles, stars on the ceiling, waking up to love songs in the morning. It looked perfect to me and the grand gestures felt so familiar too, reminding me of the presents I used to receive from my father. Consequently, being in this relationship felt like being at home, but as in my childhood, the emotional connection was missing. At the time, I didn't know myself very well, beyond focusing obsessively on how I looked.

And my partner knew how to pay a compliment! He often complimented me on my appearance and this felt familiar and soothing. What he couldn't do was empathise with the high degree of control I felt I needed, even after my relationship with my body and fitness began to improve. When I tried to share my concerns or my coping strategies, my partner would be dismissive, even while trying to comfort me.

"Oh don't be silly you look perfect!" he'd say. He couldn't cope when I tried to open up about what I struggled with emotionally. Even once I started to notice the emptiness, I stayed, and so did he. Out of convenience, out of fear? Well, possibly both.

There were signs, though, that all was not well. Like the day I found sexually explicit photos on his WhatsApp, sent to another woman a few days earlier while I'd been asleep. When I confronted him, he seemed more annoyed that I'd interrupted his work call than guilty about his betrayal, though perhaps he was embarrassed or afraid of losing me. My partner was adopted, and I was aware of the deep wound he carried from the rejection of his own birth mother.

I often used this as an excuse for his behaviour and I felt an immense responsibility to not to leave.

But I also stayed because I was scared on my own account. I felt the weight of the unspoken prescription: As a woman, by 30, I was supposed to be settled down and married with children, ticking off the boxes that defined a "successful" life. By this point, I was way over "the number" and terrified that if I left, I'd be alone and stepping into the abyss of societal judgment.

I imagined the shame I would feel in front of my parents, who dutifully married so young. I could hear their voices saying "Here we go again, you've left the man who was willing and able to provide for you!"

Looking back now, it breaks my heart that I stayed, that I thought material things could fill the emotional void inside me. It was a different location but the same story all over again. Just like my father, my partner offered material things but withheld the love and connection I craved. Just like my mother, I yelled but did not know how to speak about what we each needed.

So we carried on, first with dinners and holidays, then engagement, trying for a baby, planning a wedding… Everything that was expected of us. Things I thought I wanted. Things, perhaps, I did want. Perhaps not with him.

Certainly, I wanted to have a baby. After close to six months without any joy, I began to find it emotionally draining waiting for that positive result to show up each month. Being a few days late for my period would always spark such hope inside me, then the jolt of realising that, no, I still wasn't pregnant would tear me down.

I started to think that there was something wrong with me, so I went for tests. But no, everything was healthy. If you are a woman reading this, I don't know how you feel about it, but my experience suggests we often tend to blame ourselves, don't we? After more tests it was confirmed that the issues we were having were actually down to my partner.

Understanding that this was a lot for him to take, I played it cool for a few weeks before trying to talk to him about our options, however we didn't have the emotional connection or skill to find our way through. Instead of a conversation, I always got a "YES" because that was quicker, easier, and did not involve any negotiation. However, our second fertility consultation was a disaster, leaving us feeling like commodities. He was furious and blamed me for putting us into the situation. I shut down, completely emptied out by how the warm idea of creating a life had all but disappeared so suddenly. When he found me crying, instead of comforting me, he scolded me for being weak.

Even this was not quite the end though. Some time later, we were sitting in a classy bar in Central London when my partner said, apparently from nowhere, "Let's take it step by step. Get married and then see what happens."

This time, I didn't immediately say yes, but when I started looking at wedding venues, I saw one I had always admired and found myself starting to paint the picture of our big day.

I was hooked on "the day" and not really thinking about the reality of marriage. So, I channelled my energy into planning the wedding. I knew what my partner liked so it was not too difficult to help him to fall in love with my plans and we quickly had quite a few of the elements sorted. I started trying on dresses.

At the same time, I felt an emptiness. You know that whisper that comes from your gut? The one that we often push away because we are frightened to let it talk? My inner voice was speaking to me but I kept ignoring it even though the hollow ache I had carried into every relationship began to feel stronger as the wedding date drew closer. We argued more frequently and the emotional distance between us widened. But for some reason I clung to him harder, chasing emotional connection from someone who was unwilling or unable to give it, replaying the dynamics of my parents' relationship.

Finally, something inside me broke. I ended up in bed on a Saturday afternoon which you may recognise from this story was very out of character for me. My partner had no idea what to say to me. The next morning, I stayed away from my partner and spent time in nature because I really needed it. We met for Sunday lunch and when we sat down to order our food, he told me I was an evil person. I don't know what prompted that and I don't particularly want to but when I expressed my shock, he told me he was joking.

I remember those few seconds very well. Finally, I was at my crunch point. After an internal battle, I stood up from the table and walked away.. It was my moment of quiet clarity, when I realised that I deserved better. It wasn't easy, and the fear didn't disappear overnight, but for the first time, I chose *me*. Not the person I thought I needed to be to earn love, but the person I truly was, however imperfect. It was the right thing to do, even though calling off the wedding and giving back my engagement ring cut me into pieces.

Act Four: Living for Myself and Stronger Than Ever

In the early days after our breakup, I was boiling over with the need to name all the things my ex-partner had done wrong. I believe this is a normal and natural phase of any break-up, a necessary stage for making some sense of everything and finding a way forward into the space beyond.

However, for the first time, I also faced into a hard truth: Again and again, through my adult life, I based all my worth on the physical appearance of my body, choosing partners who couldn't give me the love and connection I desired because I didn't believe I was worthy of it! I had been sabotaging myself, unconsciously recreating the dynamics of my childhood in an effort to make sense of my pain. It was a sharp awakening, but it was also the catalyst for the most profound transformation of my life. I knew if I wanted my life to be different I needed to be different. *Nothing changes if nothing changes* became my mantra and remains a favourite quote to this day. It's an idea I would like to offer also to you.

This was not an easy time but although I had tears in my eyes, I held my head up high. I knew I had chosen to value myself and that I had more within me to see me through. I did not distract myself with quick fixes like alcohol, drugs, or sex, and this time, I did not take refuge, either, in the numb effects of food.

Instead, I really turned my attention inward, and I would recommend anyone else in crisis to do the same. I looked after my body as well as I could. I found solitude in nature. Even though, at first, I was petrified of my own company at first, I knew I had to learn how to be alone.

During this process, being able to be active was central to my recovery. I will forever be grateful to fitness. It literally saved me in those dark moments and continues to do so, today.

For the very first time I saw my fitness regime for what it really is – a set of methods for building resilience, strength, and robust health, that can help with finding a strong community and that can develop the inner resolve needed to jump over any obstacle life presents. This time, I also knew I could not find my way into a new story on my own. I surrendered my illusions of being independent and I asked for help. Thankfully, I found people around me who were willing to be there for me, without judgement, to listen and to offer love. I am grateful for every single one of them. (If you're reading this, you know who you are.)

With the help of a therapist, I began to unravel the layers of my pain and understand the roots of my struggles. I saw how my childhood experiences had shaped my beliefs about love, worthiness, and connection. I learned that I had been living and loving from a place of fear and scarcity, believing that I had to earn love and approval by being perfect, by looking a certain way, or by taking care of others at the expense of my own needs.

I realised that I had been living according to a script that wasn't mine and that if I wanted to find true happiness, I needed to write a new one. My own.

I have been learning to love and accept myself, to forgive myself for my mistakes, and to embrace my imperfections. It has meant redefining my relationship with food, with my body, and with my emotions.

I began to see food not as a source of comfort or punishment but as nourishment for my body and soul. I started to treat my body with kindness and respect, to listen to its needs, and to honour its limits. And I learned to feel my emotions fully, to express them without fear or shame, and to let them guide me rather than control me. I challenged my 'healthy' unhealthy narratives and beliefs.

I invested in myself, and worked with an incredible coach, Marco, who is behind this extraordinary project. My hope is that by opening up about my own struggles and triumphs, I can inspire others to start over, to rewrite their own stories, and to create lives that are true reflections of who they are and what they deserve.

This profound shift in my perspective led me to a new calling: to help other women through fitness who, like me, have felt frustrated and lost. Who have found themselves at rock bottom and don't know how to climb back up. Who have struggled with their body image and food.

Spending so much time and energy on controlling everything to the smallest bite, missing out on special moments. I want you to know that there is a different way to be healthy and strong.

A way where you look after your body with movement, and food. A way where you can push yourself on the days where you don't feel like it, but at the same time dial back down because your body asks for rest. With no fear or guilt. This can be your way to freedom. Freedom to move, eat and live the way you want. No more fitting anyone else's box. You can be strong, sexy, smart… all at the same time.

In the end, I can honestly say that I will be forever grateful to my ex-partner. The good and the bad that we experienced together is what has prepared me to guide other women on their paths to strength, self-care and robust health.

I want to share the lessons I learned, to empower women to break free from their own cycles of self-sabotage and to reclaim their lives with courage and confidence.

I want to help women to fall in love with their bodies and to stop trying to control everything.

I am part of the movement that shouts to women that they are more than their bodies and I will be loud about this so that you, your daughter, sister, and all the younger generations can have a safe space to care for their bodies, minds and souls - not from a place of fear, but love. So they don't associate worth with being skinny. So they can be free to be who they want. But most importantly, they are driven by care and not punishment.

To any woman who feels she has to look smaller, who feels that needs to fit inside a box, who has been told that she is too much in any way, shape or form … Know, that you are not. You are allowed to be who you want. With a body that feels strong and sexy to you.

Standing up and starting over is not about forgetting who you were, but about becoming who you were always meant to be. It's about choosing to live a life that reflects your true self, not the expectations or fears of others. It's about rewriting the script, one page at a time, and creating a story that is truly your own. This is my message to you: It is never too late to start over. It is never too late to heal. It is never too late to become the hero of your own story.

So, here's to new beginnings, to rewriting our stories, and to becoming the heroes of our own lives. Here's to breaking free from the past and stepping boldly into the future. Here's to starting over.

To the unyielding courage in all of us, may we rise, may we shine, and may we live our lives as women we were born to be. Let us become *Once in a Lifetime* kind of women!

To connect with Radomira scan the QR code

ABOUT THE AUTHOR

RADOMIRA SUNAVCOVA

SCAN TO KNOW MORE

Radomira Sunavcova is a fierce Women's Health and Well-Being Coach on a mission to help women break free from societal chains and reclaim their strength, confidence, and sensuality. Having overcome years of restrictive diets and self-doubt, she discovered true power comes from care, not control. Through her bold 12 Weeks: Be the Unstoppable programme, Radomira empowers women to shed fear, embrace resilience, and celebrate their bodies unapologetically. Her work redefines health as a vibrant celebration of self-worth and vitality.

START OVER VOL 1

CHAPTER

7

Rising from the Ashes:

The Unyielding Courage of a Broken Soul

GAURAV RAJWANSHI

(Shattered Dreams)

The path to success is never a straight line, but mine seemed like an endless series of jagged cliffs, plunging valleys, and sharp turns that I never saw coming in time. I was born and brought up on the grounds of a small town in northern India where dreams felt like distant stars – beautiful, yes, but always out of reach and silence often felt like the safest option (at least to me). Over time, I mastered the art of becoming invisible. There were moments—cruel, defining moments—when doubt and rejection chiselled away at my confidence until all that was left was a hollow version of myself. This is the way I remember everything.

Growing up, I didn't even know what it meant to be introverted. The word itself was foreign to me, but the feeling wasn't. The environment I grew up in was anything but encouraging. It was harsh and unforgiving—a place where vulnerability was met with cruelty. But despite the constant barrage of negativity, beneath the scars and bruises, a tiny flame flickered. Small, weak, but stubbornly alive.

That spark led me to sign up for a performance at school when I was in the sixth grade (year 6) or maybe I had been pushed to do so. The fear was overwhelming, but somehow, I took those ten steps to come onto that humongous stage. As I stood on the stage with a mic in front of me, the heat of a thousand eyes bore down on me. I could hear my heart catching up to my brain. My throat went dry, my palms slick with sweat. After a few minutes of starting my performance, the recital of a poem, the words I'd rehearsed, over and over in the confines of my room, vanished into the void and all that was left was a profound suffocating silence.

"Look at him," someone sneered into the mic, *"This is the future of our city, our country? Shame on you."* It was my Head Teacher — his words slicing through the silence like a dagger, embarrassing me in front of over 500 students, teachers, school staff and in my mind at that time – the whole world. Laughter echoed through the hall as my face burned with humiliation. Tears filled my eyes, blurring my vision, as I thought, *'Please, let this end. Just let me disappear'*. But instead, the jeers only grew louder and I stood there, frozen, trapped in that moment of raw shame.

That night, I cried myself to sleep, the echo of those words swirled in my head like a cruel mantra -*'Shame on you'*, making me wonder if I'd be anything more than a disgrace. I tossed and turned, wishing for the night to swallow me whole, for the world to forget what had happened.

But deep down, it was impossible to forget. It turned into a repetitive thought, an obsessive thought and eventually it turned into an invisible mental scar that would stay with me, a mark that wouldn't fade with time.

Even as I lay there in the dark, the shame tightening its grip around me, there was a small spark, barely there, inside me. A whisper of defiance. *You survived,* it said. *You stood up there. You didn't run.* And though it was small, that whisper was enough. Enough to make me think, maybe—just maybe—I could survive this too. Maybe this was the last time.

But the school offered no second chances. For three long years, I remained in that place, never getting another opportunity to prove myself. I carried my inferiority like a boulder, crushing my spirit a little more with every passing day. It was the small moments, the lingering looks, the half-whispered gossips- that chipped away my confidence completely by the time I moved to a new school. There too the chances remained elusive and two more years passed without a single opportunity to step onto a stage. The voices of doubt were everywhere— neighbours whispered, family members scolded, and worst of all, my own mind taunted me, telling me I was worthless. I vividly remember a time when, at an event, I saw a boy (almost of my age) dressed impeccably. Nothing special, yet, his appearance alone was so intimidating that it made me feel inferior. I avoided him at all costs, convinced that I wasn't even worthy of standing in his presence or in anybody's presence who is well dressed, well-spoken or good looking.

It was during those days when I started listening to the legendary voice of a great Bollywood singer Kishore Kumar. His songs, timeless and immortal, soothed my wounded soul, every single time. I don't know exactly when, but I started contemplating that even though he was gone, his voice lived on—a legacy, eternal and untouchable. A thought took root in my mind: *What if I could leave something behind that would outlive me? Something that would stand the test of time, like Kishore's voice?* At fifteen or sixteen, it was just a fleeting notion, but it stayed with me. And kept going deeper and stronger. Also, music itself started to heal and inspire me, without me even trying to sing or play it.

(The Long Dark Road)

My life soon took an unexpected turn as I entered College (we used to call it Polytechnique). For the first time in life, now I had to commute to another city —a bustling metropolis full of strangers. Each day felt like a battle I was destined to lose. My self-esteem was so low that even the simplest things, like finding a seat on the bus, became a daunting task. I preferred standing, clutching my bag like a lifeline, terrified that sitting next to someone, especially a girl, would invite judgment. My mind spun wild fantasies of ridicule and gossip, imagining eyes watching my every move. I would rather endure aching legs and a pounding heart than face the imagined consequences of simply sitting down. Because of a fear that someone might say something. Where was this fear coming from? Have a guess.

But life has a way of pushing you, even when you're not ready. And so, one day, a girl from my class who used to take the same bus as me, noticed my perpetual standing. I had seen her around but never really shared a conversation with her. The bus was packed as usual, and once again, there was only one seat available— this time, right next to her.

"No, don't sit. They'll make fun of you." I said to myself, looking everywhere else but towards that empty seat until she looked up at me and, most casually, asked, *"Why are you standing? Come sit here, sit down."*

Her words were so simple, yet they threw me completely off balance. My first instinct was to decline, to keep standing as if it was no big deal but there was something in her tone, something humble yet commanding. Against every fiber of my being, I took that seat.

"Thankyou" I mumbled, not sure whether she could even hear it. A wave of discomfort washed over me. I could feel their eyes on me, burning through my skin. *Were they judging*

me, or was this all in my head? My mind raced, conjuring up every possible judgment people could throw my way. But to my surprise, nothing happened. No snickers, no stares—just the hum of the engine and the city outside. It was such a small thing, occupying an empty seat, but to me, it felt like a rebellion against the crippling fear that had held me hostage for so long. Later we became really good friends and always used to sit together on the bus. But it took a long time to acquire that courage.

During those days, music continued to be my peace until one day this music changed everything. It was an ordinary day in our polytechnic lecture, and the professor, clearly not in the mood to take a lecture, asked *"Is there anyone who wants to come up and perform or say —anything at all?"*.

I saw a guy raise his hand and he started singing. I don't know what came over me, but before I knew it, my hand was up too. It was as if something inside me had snapped. I wasn't thinking, I wasn't planning—I just acted. "Can I go next please", I said and walked to the front of the class, and sang a song. To this day, I don't remember how well I sang or what the reaction was. What I do remember, though, is that there was no mocking voice, no sneering comment, no judgment. For the first time in years, I was on stage (almost) and the only sound I heard was my own voice and a few claps afterwards. It was no less than winning the world.

When I returned to my seat, I felt something I hadn't felt in years—pride. It wasn't about how well I had sung; it was about the fact that I had sung. Ok, let me say this, it was not about the song at all. It was about me facing the audience again after 5 years and not forgetting my words and finishing what I started. Although it took 5 long years, my mission was accomplished. At that moment, I realized that I had the power to change my narrative and to rise above the voices that had kept me down for so long.

In hindsight today it feels like that small victory was the beginning of my transformation. I started taking steps—small at first, but significant in their impact. I participated in more performances, not just at class level but in informal gatherings with friends. I was slowly rebuilding the confidence that had been shattered years before. I had tasted what it felt like to be seen and appreciated, and I wanted more of it. Luckily, I met a lot of supportive friends, classmates as well. I'm so grateful for all of them.

Around this time, something monumental entered my life—computers. It was the year of 1996, and while my peers flaunted shiny new bikes, music systems, new clothes and were hanging out all the time, I was in my own world, saving every penny to buy my first computer. But I didn't just buy it. I built it—piece by piece. The memory of assembling it is etched into my soul, every component clicking into place like a manifestation of hope. As the screen flickered to life, so did something deep within me. This wasn't just a machine; it was the physical embodiment of my ability to create, to bring something from nothing into the world. It was proof—tangible proof—that I had worth, that I was capable of more than I ever thought possible.

With every keystroke, every software tweak, I began to see myself through a new lens. I wasn't just the quiet, overlooked kid anymore. I was becoming someone who could solve problems, someone who could master skills that others found difficult. The endless possibilities in the world of computers consumed me—whether it was tinkering with software, diving into graphic design, or simply getting lost in the digital landscapes of video games. I was about to become big in my tiny world.

Soon word got out. People started coming to me for help. *"You know computers, right?"* they'd ask, their voices filled with a respect I wasn't used to hearing. I felt valued. I wasn't invisible anymore. Slowly, I built a reputation—one of those 'go-to' guys when it came to anything about computers. It wasn't just validation. It was the beginning of a new narrative—one where I mattered.

But even as I began to rise, as my confidence started to blossom, the voices of doubt from my past were never completely silent. People who knew me since childhood still whispered cruelly, unable to see the person I was becoming *"You're good for nothing,"*. And while their words stung, something inside me had shifted. This time, I knew better. I was no longer defined by their small-mindedness. Their dismissive comments became background noises as I carved out my path.

After 3 years of college, I entered university to get a degree in computer engineering. I carried this renewed sense of purpose with me like armour. I wasn't there to make friends or impress anyone. I was there to learn, to master my craft, to become the best version of myself. Or maybe I was trying hard to stay big in my tiny world of computers. But despite my resolve, life had a way of pulling me out of my comfort zone.

After my first year, an event was announced, where students were invited to step into the spotlight. I watched as my classmates eagerly signed up to debate, to perform, to showcase their talents. I felt that familiar tug—that spark from my polytechnic days. *Could I do this again? Could I stand on a stage and be more than just the quiet, introverted computer guy?*

So, I signed up. Without hesitation, I put my name down for choreography and a play. I was even surprised by my decision. On the day of the event, my heart pounded in my chest, echoing the same fear I'd felt years ago. But this time, something was different. This time, I was ready.

I danced with every ounce of energy I had, and when it was time to deliver my lines in the play, I spoke with a confidence I didn't know I possessed. The response was overwhelming—applause, cheers, voices calling out my name. For the first time in my life, I felt like I truly belonged. I wasn't just a student of computer engineering anymore. I was someone who could command attention, someone who had earned respect in more ways than one. Someone even gave me the title of showman (someone who can put on great shows on stage). I must also mention that it took me two months of prep work and a lot of rehearsals with my team to put this show together. In short, life has no shortcuts.

But as I soared, the shadows of my past weren't far behind. The voices I thought I had left behind resurfaced one more time, when I failed a subject. One professor, who had never believed in me, looked at me with disdain. His words, laced with venom, pierced through my growing confidence. *"You'll never amount to anything."*

Those words were not new. They were a punch to the gut. But this time, I was not the same old Gaurav, so, I didn't crumble. I couldn't and I wouldn't. I took his words and turned them into fuel. With every ounce of determination, I threw myself into my studies, determined to prove him wrong. And when the results came in, I not only passed—I scored highest. I waited for the recognition, for the moment of redemption, but instead, his words came down on me harder: *"It's a disgrace to our education system that someone like you can score so well."*

It was another dagger to the heart, sharper than anything I had ever felt. *Was I truly deserving of my success, or had it all been a fluke?* The doubts crept back in, unravelling the confidence I had fought so hard to build. But even as the world seemed to turn against me, I clung to one thing—the memory of that stage, the applause, the cheers. The undeniable truth that I had risen before, and I could rise again. I think I was able to see the rollercoaster patterns of life.

Slowly, steadily, I began to see that success wasn't defined by the judgments of others. It wasn't even defined by the failures or setbacks I faced. Success was defined by my resilience—by my ability to keep moving forward, even when everything seemed to be working against me. And my ability to bounce back, much stronger; every time.

This period of my life wasn't just about proving others wrong. It was about proving something to myself. It was about stripping away the layers of doubt, the expectations that others had placed on me, and finding the core of who I truly was. With every step forward, I discovered new strength within myself. I took risks, ventured into the unknown, wrote plays, choreographed musicals, and performed on stages I never thought I'd stand on.

And with each new challenge, the chains of my past loosened. The quiet, introverted boy who had once feared the spotlight was slowly transforming into someone unafraid to take a stand, to speak up, to fail—and to rise again. It wasn't just about succeeding anymore. It was about becoming someone who knew their worth. Someone who didn't need anyone else's approval to believe in themselves.

Looking back now, I see that every struggle, every setback, every harsh word was an essential part of my journey. And as I walked across that university stage, some community stages, degree in hand, I knew that the journey wasn't over. Far from it. The world was waiting, and I was ready—stronger, more determined, and more resilient than ever before.

(Rebirth)

After university, I dived headfirst into the corporate world, eager to make my mark. I had skills, knowledge, and a burning desire to succeed, but I quickly discovered that the corporate landscape was a different beast altogether. It wasn't just about what you knew or how hard you worked; it was about navigating office politics, dealing with difficult personalities, and constantly proving your worth.

I threw myself into my work, determined to climb the ladder. The long hours, the relentless pressure, the constant need to outdo myself—all of it took a toll. I was succeeding in the ways that mattered on paper. I was earning good money, rising through the ranks, and gaining the recognition I had always craved. But with each promotion, with each new responsibility, the weight on my shoulders grew heavier. I was so focused on the next goal, the next achievement, the next milestone in my career that my health deteriorated, my joy faded, and the achievements I had once dreamed of felt hollow.

Time passed in a blur of meetings, deadlines, and late nights at the office. I had become so consumed by the pursuit of success that I had lost sight of what truly mattered.

Years later, I found myself sitting in a hospital room, holding my newborn daughter in my arms. Her tiny fingers curled around mine, her soft breaths the only sound in the stillness. It was a moment that changed me in ways I hadn't expected. Suddenly, all the things I had been chasing—wealth, success, recognition—seemed insignificant compared to the responsibility of being a father. I wasn't just living for myself anymore. I wanted to give her the best life possible, to protect her, to ensure she grew up safe and happy. But with that realization came a new kind of fear.

We were living in New Delhi, a city I had called home for my entire life. As I looked at my daughter, my heart clenched with fear, one that gnawed at me from the inside. I'd watch her while she was asleep, her tiny chest rising and falling in a peaceful rhythm, and the anxiety would hit me, hard and fast. Delhi always had its challenges, but now it felt different. Recent incidents in the news painted a picture of a city that was increasingly unsafe, especially for females. The streets outside our window, once filled with the hum of life, now seemed hostile to me. Every distant sound—the honk of a car, the muffled voices of passers by—felt like a threat. I couldn't shake the sense of danger that hung in the air, thick and oppressive, making it hard to breathe. The thought of her growing up here, vulnerable to all the things I couldn't control, twisted in my chest until I could barely stand it. Delhi was the same, but my mind was not. My childhood-related insecurities and fears took a new shape this time.

I tried to brush it off, telling myself it was just my mind playing tricks, that I was letting fear get the best of me. But the anxiety wasn't just a fleeting thought—it was a constant presence, hovering over me every moment of every day. I couldn't escape it. It wrapped around me like a heavy blanket, making my breaths shallow, my nights sleepless. I found myself pacing the house, unable to sit still, consumed by the "what-ifs." *What if something happened to her? What if I couldn't protect her? What if this city took away the one thing that mattered most to me?*

I started waking up in cold sweats, the images from my nightmares mixing with the reality outside. The walls of our home began to feel too close, the air too thick. I couldn't stop the thoughts—the endless loop of worst-case scenarios playing in my mind. Every time I kissed her goodnight, the weight of what I couldn't protect her from became unbearable.

The breaking point came one afternoon when I was watching her play in the living room. She was laughing, carefree, her tiny hands reaching for her toys, blissfully unaware of the world outside. And then, without warning, the thought hit me like a wave crashing over my head: *I can't do this anymore. I can't raise her here.*

It wasn't just a thought—it was a realization so profound that it nearly knocked the wind out of me. I walked over to the window and stared out at the sprawling city, the skyline blurring as my eyes filled with tears. The familiar sights, the crowded streets, the chaotic hum of Delhi—all of it suddenly felt foreign. This was no longer my home. It had become a place I feared, a place I couldn't imagine my daughter growing up in. The city I had once embraced was now suffocating me. I knew then that it was time. Time to leave behind the only life I had ever known. Time to start over somewhere new, somewhere that felt safe.

I explored for opportunities in the UK and the USA, and luckily got something from both countries. I chose to start a new life in the UK with nothing but the hope that this would be the right choice for my family.

As the plane ascended into the sky, I gripped the armrest so tight my knuckles turned white. In my head, the questions screamed: *'Is this it? Will we make it here, or am I setting us up for failure?'* The pit in my stomach refused to settle, even as the clouds swallowed Delhi below until I felt a soft palm on my clenched fists. *"Don't worry, we'll get through,"* my wife said most ardently as if she could read my mind.

Soon enough, we landed in the UK with our one-year-old daughter, with almost no money and a job which did not help me provide for my family. In India, we had been doing well financially, but the cost of maintaining our lifestyle had drained much of our savings. Now, in a new country, we found ourselves starting all over from scratch. It was a humbling experience, to say the least.

For months, we were graciously hosted by friends, shifting from one home to the next, often spending nights on living room floors. The instability was exhausting, but we pressed on, knowing this was a temporary hardship. I spent my days job hunting, but the market was tough, and opportunities were few and far between. There were moments when I questioned whether I had made the right decision, or whether I had jeopardized my family's future with this drastic move.

But despite the difficulties, my wife's unwavering support held me stronger than ever. Every now and then when I carried within myself the burden of rejection, she stood right behind me telling me- *"We didn't come this far for you to carry this burden alone. I believe in you, more than anything. We are in this together. Only You're not doing this just for us. We're doing it for each other, for our family."* I knew I had to make it work, not just for myself, but for my wife and daughter.

One day a friend called me and said, "My company would hire you for a good package, if you can crack an interview based on new technology called Scala". Wow! Money was great but I had never heard of Scala before, yet, I had nothing to lose. For two weeks, I immersed myself completely in learning this new technology. I spent every moment studying, sleeping or eating, fully determined to master it.

When I finally felt ready, my friend put me in front of his team. They liked what they saw, and finally, after learning and struggling for 6 months, I was offered a decent job to provide for my family. It was a turning point for us. We moved out of shared accommodation and into our place. We were truly beginning to settle in.

As the years passed, I continued to grow in my career, working hard and eventually gaining British citizenship.

With that newfound stability, I began to explore the idea of entrepreneurship. The corporate world had taught me a lot, but it had also taken its toll. I knew I wanted something more, something that would allow me to have a greater impact and create something meaningful.

As I began exploring entrepreneurship, I started to see the bigger picture. I wasn't just interested in making money; I wanted to create something that would have a lasting impact. I wanted to build something that would stand the test of time, just like the voice of Kishore Kumar who had inspired me so many years ago. I started small, taking on projects that allowed me to use my skills and experience in meaningful ways. Slowly but surely, I began to build something that I could be proud of. I am so grateful, that my love of music was passed on to my daughter as well and for 5 years of her childhood, I could homeschool her so that we could take full control of her education and she could pursue music full time. Life has really come so far. Bigger and Beautiful.

(Epilogue)

Today, as I return home from a busy day in the office to the soft melody of my daughter, Aadya playing the piano- I can't help but reflect on how these melodies, once a lifeline in the moments of uncertainty, now serve as a bridge between my past and present. Nothing has moved me more than watching my daughter, **Aadya Rajwanshi**, grow and flourish. She even appeared on the blind audition of **The Voice Kids UK**, where all four coaches Pixie, Paloma, Will.i.am and Danny pressed the buzzer and turned their chair for her. She chose Pixie. Which was a proud moment that brought happy tears to my eyes. Seeing her stand on that stage, brimming with confidence, brought back memories of my own journey—the courage it takes to step forward despite fear. At the time of writing this story, that video of her has 19 Million views on YouTube.

You can watch it here: https://youtu.be/XVfyxyKSoco

Now, she's taken her creativity a step further, running her own YouTube channel, and I've found myself stepping into new roles—learning photography, videography, video editing, and mastering social media—all so I can support her in this exciting venture. It's been a rewarding experience, and it's taught me that no matter how far we go in life, there's always something new to learn and new ways to grow.

Today, I am living a life beyond anything I could have imagined—a life I once wouldn't have dared to dream of. And, it's not just about my personal success; it's about the people I've been able to help, the lives I've touched, and the impact we're making together. Through my work, I've had the privilege to design courses, develop programs, and create products on Leadership, Business and Digital Transformation, Agile and recently AI as well—helping thousands of people across the UK, USA, India, Australia, and beyond. Additionally, my passion for innovation and technology has led me to write two books with the following working titles —" **AI-Powered Scrum Mastery: Unlocking New Levels of Agility and Efficiency"** and **"AI-Powered Product Ownership: Mastering Product Development with Precision"**—where I explore how AI is reshaping Agile ways of working and driving success in the modern workplace. Both books are ready to publish and by the time you will read this, they should be available for purchase on major book platforms.

I took a leap of faith, just before the world was upended by the COVID-19 pandemic and started new ventures with colleagues and friends who shared my passion for innovation. Together, we built businesses that generated millions annually in the last 3 years. But it's not just about financial success. The real satisfaction comes from the impact we've made. These businesses aren't just a source of revenue—they're a source of opportunity. We've created employment for many people, given them a chance to build better lives for themselves and their families, and empowered them to become the best versions of themselves. That, to me, is the true reward.

By this stage in my life, I've learned a lesson that success isn't just about climbing the corporate ladder or collecting accolades. It's deeper than that. True success is about living with intention, clarity, and a sense of purpose. It's about understanding the pillars that hold up a meaningful life: **health, wealth, and relationships**, all rooted in the foundation of **spirituality**.

Health, I've learned, is non-negotiable. It is the bedrock of everything we strive for. No amount of wealth or recognition can replace it. I learned that the hard way, pushing myself too far, only to realize that without health, nothing else matters. You cannot pour from an empty cup, and when your body or mind fails, no amount of success can fill that void.

Wealth, on the other hand, brings comfort and security, but it is not the destination. Used wisely, it can build a life of freedom and purpose. It's not about accumulation for the sake of it; it's about what you do with it, how you use it to create meaning and value.

And then, there are **relationships**—with family, friends, and colleagues. These connections breathe life into everything we do. Achievements hold little weight if you have no one to share them with, no one to grow alongside, no one to remind you of who you are when the world gets too loud.

But these three pillars—health, wealth, and relationships—only stand strong when anchored by **spirituality**. For me, spirituality is more than a belief system; it's a way of understanding that we are part of something far greater than ourselves. It's about waking up each day with gratitude, recognizing our place in the world, and finding peace within. It's about giving back, contributing to something beyond just material success.

This realization became the cornerstone of how I approached life, both personally and professionally. **Balance**, I discovered, was the key. Life is not about chasing one thing at the expense of another. It's about understanding that when one pillar shakes, the others can keep you steady, as long as your foundation—your spirituality—remains intact. These days, I am working hard on the health pillar as life keeps on pushing me out of balance and I need to bring back the balance by shifting priorities from pillar to pillar. In this journey of life, there is no finish line where everything suddenly becomes perfect, forever. It's about learning, failing, bouncing back, and starting over again. And that's okay.

To anyone reading this, who feels lost, broken, or defeated, I want you to know this: **You have the strength within you to rise from the ashes.** Life may have knocked you down, but you have the power to stand up again, stronger and more resilient than before. Ashes of your past do not define your future unless you let them. Each day is an opportunity to rebuild, to reshape your story, and to become the person you've wanted to be.

Looking back, I see how every struggle, every setback, and every victory has shaped me into who I am today. The shy, introverted boy who once trembled at the thought of speaking up has grown into someone who isn't afraid to take risks, to fail, and to rise again. Every challenge I faced, every doubt I battled, has added to the person I've become. I wouldn't change a thing from my past, even if I could.

As you reach the end of this chapter, I want you to remember something important: your story isn't over. No matter where you are or what's happening, there are still so many possibilities ahead. The tough moments don't define you - they help you grow. You can START OVER at any time.

If any part of this chapter inspired you, take a step towards your dreams. Whether it's starting something new, changing how you think, or believing in yourself again - the time to act is now.

To stay updated with my latest work and receive exclusive insights, scan the QR code below to subscribe to my newsletter.

You'll get updates on leadership, AI, and personal growth delivered directly to you.

ABOUT THE AUTHOR

GAURAV RAJWANSHI

SCAN TO KNOW MORE

Gaurav Rajwanshi is a business leader and transformation strategist passionate about guiding organizations through complex change. With extensive experience across industries, he leverages innovation, AI, Lean, and agile methodologies to drive impactful results. Gaurav's journey is rooted in resilience, emphasizing the human stories behind every challenge and success. Committed to empowering people and businesses, he fosters growth by aligning technical and human potential. Whether leading transformations or hosting workshops, his focus remains on creating meaningful impact.

START OVER VOL 1

CHAPTER

8

The Volcano That Burned My Home

And Ignited My Soul's Flame

ESTHER HEESE

"Embrace uncertainty. Some of the most beautiful chapters in our lives won't have a title until much later."

— Bob Goff

Looking back on my life at 61, I see a journey marked by sudden, unpredictable life changes—each one plunging me into a phase of uncertainty that stirred a deep-seated fear. For years, I tried to manage that fear with tense, controlling behaviour, convinced it would keep me safe.

But trying to control life is not only exhausting—it's futile. It's like trying to hold an inflated air mattress underwater. No matter how hard you press down, one corner always escapes, popping up where you least expect it. It's a constant struggle that leaves you drained, with no real victory in sight.

Thankfully, over the years, I've learned that when life throws me onto shaky ground, I can find balance with flexible legs, rather than clinging desperately to the handrail of predictability.

Are you ready to explore how I transformed my overwhelming fear of uncertainty into the art of gracefully dancing with the unknown?

Seeds of Anxiety
Torn from the Nest: My Childhood Battle with Abandonment

I was barely out of my mother's womb when I was first separated from my family for two months. This separation became an annual routine because my father's profession required him to travel during the summer, and with four older sisters already at home, managing a baby became too challenging. As the fifth child, I was taken to my grandmother's every summer until I was four. While my grandmother undoubtedly cared for me lovingly, the repeated, abrupt change of caregivers—something a toddler cannot understand or process—created a significant disruption in my attachment patterns.

When I was one, proudly taking my first steps, a severe stomach flu sent me to the children's hospital for several weeks. My parents came to visit, but when it was time for them to leave, I clung to them, crying desperately—too young to understand and too terrified to let go.

"The child needs calm to heal," the doctor insisted. They forbade my parents from visiting, fearing that emotional goodbyes would be too stressful. But I was left alone, too little to understand why they had gone and too frightened to find any sense of calm. I cried until I couldn't anymore, sinking into silence—not because I was at peace, but because I had no strength left. The fear stayed with me, unhealed and buried deep.

What this truly means emotionally for a toddler only became clear to me when I closely observed my own son at that age. The way he would cry in fear, even if I was just closing the bathroom door and he couldn't bear waiting outside alone, showed me the depth of a child's need for security and connection.

The Day My Sun Vanished: Desperately Missing My Father

"Now we have to tell the little one that Dad is moving out," my mother whispered to one of my older sisters. I overheard the words, but at seven years old, I didn't fully understand what they meant. As the youngest of five daughters, I had been shielded from my parents' impending separation. No one had prepared me for what was coming.

Minutes later, my father stood in the hallway with two suitcases at his feet. The shock hit me like a cold wave. My father—the sun in my life, my emotional anchor, my patient and inspiring violin teacher—was leaving. This was the man who, after returning from the opera where he was singing, would always check in on us at night, often bringing us something to drink. How could he just walk out and not come back?

I remember that farewell hug as if it were yesterday. Terrified, I clung to his neck, trying to keep him from leaving, so rigid with shock that I couldn't even cry. As he gently pried me away, I felt my world collapse around me. He walked out the door, and I didn't know when, or if, he would ever return. For weeks, maybe months, I cried myself to sleep, hoping he would come back and make everything okay again.

A year later, my father did return, and my parents remarried. If I had known that, the pain of missing him wouldn't have been so overwhelming. But the uncertainty, the endless waiting, left a lasting mark on my nervous system—a wound that continued to ache with the fear of loss and instability.

Crashing into Heartbreak: A First Love Lost in Silence

At fourteen, I experienced my first love—a blend of excitement, tenderness, and a sense of being uplifted. But one evening at the youth center, as I cheerfully approached the boy I had been dating for four months, I saw him holding another girl in his arms. It felt like slamming into an invisible glass wall.

I stood there, frozen, my heart pounding and my breath catching in my throat. I couldn't think, couldn't speak—just paralyzed by a mix of jealousy, confusion, and self-doubt.

Before he could see me, I turned and slipped out of the club, hoping to disappear into the night. As I hid in my bed at home, tears streaming down my face, I waited desperately for his call. But weeks passed, and I never heard from him.

This seemingly simple heartbreak reinforced my deep-rooted fear of uncertainty. Once again, I was confronted with the agonizing silence and absence of closure, echoing the abandonment I had felt as a young child. Little did I realize that these early experiences were shaping a pattern—a pattern that would later influence how I dealt with loss and change in all its forms.

My Fruitless Attempt At Control

The shock of these various experiences burned itself into my nervous system. This vague, subliminal feeling of facing and fearing uncertainty became part of my personality. I began to be chronically "on guard".

I developed an inner detective. An entity whose job it was to recognize the smallest signs of a threatening change as early as possible. I wanted to gain at least a small time advantage over the inevitable. A desperate attempt to prepare myself well in advance.

I grew a strong need for control - with all the reprehensible excesses of clandestine no-go's like secretly listening to conversations at the door, snooping through private papers and scanning my partner's phone without permission.

And of course I found things that worried me. And then? How was I supposed to deal with it if I couldn't openly admit where I got some of the information? My anxious thoughts spread like poison in every cell - trapped in a lonely cocoon of shame about my totally unacceptable controlling behaviour.

My attempt to control my environment did not bring me any real inner peace. I was subliminally nervous, suspicious and anxious.

A mother's nightmare

At the age of 25, I became a mother, cradling my beautiful baby with all the joy and love I could imagine. But just a year later, our happiness was shaken when my little one fell seriously ill with a rare disease.

"We need to go to the hospital. Can you see how he keeps tilting his little head back?" I urged my husband, and we hurried to the nearest hospital with our beloved one-year-old.

One examination after another, but still no answers. Each test brought a mix of hope and disappointment as the doctors searched for the cause. Endless waiting, endless not knowing —it felt unbearable. My husband and I stayed in the hospital day and night, refusing to leave our son's side. The uncertainty —that was the hardest part.

Time seemed to stand still, each second stretching painfully as we waited for answers. And then, after what felt like an eternity, we got a diagnosis: polio. Polio is a viral infection that attacks the nerves in the spine, potentially causing muscle weakness and paralysis. In severe cases, it can lead to permanent disability or even death if it affects the muscles used for breathing. A disease that hadn't been seen in our country for years. The shock of it even made headlines in some newspapers.

But even with a diagnosis, the fear didn't end. Now, we had to face the unknown aftermath—the damage the virus might leave behind. Each day, we checked his muscles and reflexes, praying for signs of recovery, fearing what might be permanent. Our nerves were constantly frayed, swinging between hope and dread. Every moment was agony as we helplessly watched, unable to control what would come next.

In this situation, my usual urge to control and manage the outer world was utterly powerless. All we could do was hold on, riding the relentless wave of fear and uncertainty, hoping our little boy would pull through.

He did make it, though with paralyzed muscles in his left leg. We had finally emerged from the painful and overwhelming uncertainty. Now, we could face the concrete reality and take whatever steps were necessary to provide him with the support he needed.

Insight to Impact

When I was 28, one of my best friends began attending therapeutic self-development seminars focused on

"Healing the Wounded Inner Child," which combined depth psychology with meditation - an approach known as Transpersonal Psychology. From there she brought back insights about inner dynamics that I found super fascinating and soaked up like a sponge. I recognized my own thoughts, feelings, and behaviors in many of her vivid descriptions, igniting a deep passion to explore my emotional and mental inner world and its impact on my connections with others.

A short time later I was sitting in one of these seminars myself - right in the front row, eager to understand and absorb every little detail.

That was the beginning of an intense journey of healing, exploration and learning that fascinates me to this day. I have even followed my inner calling to turn this passion into a profession and to pass on everything that I experience as healing by becoming a therapist, couples-coach and mindfulness teacher.

The Connection-Triangle as the Antidote to Fear

The insights I gained during that time led me to what I now call "The Connection Triangle."

Fear often stems from a sense of isolation and disconnection. By fostering connection in three key areas—within ourselves, with others, and with our Soul—we can effectively release fear and cultivate a sense of safety and belonging.

1. **Connecting to oneself (intrapersonal)**

   It was only through self-exploration and meditation that I found a way to calm my inner tension.

In seminars and individual therapeutic sessions I increasingly discovered the different parts of my inner landscape. I began to realize the tragic dynamics of my controlling behavior that was an attempt to save me from another unexpected experience of shock. I found out how to lovingly embrace and calm my terrified "Inner Child".

Finally I was ready to stop running away from my unsettling feelings and instead slow down and deeply connect with myself. There is a way to mindfully embrace feelings within the body, allowing them to be integrated healthily without being overwhelmed by their intensity.

Key insight

Being connected to ourselves by becoming aware of our feelings, thoughts, impulses, needs and boundaries can be turned into a doorway to self-love and confidence. Increased self-contact allows us to understand and address our fears rather than be overwhelmed by them. Becoming aware of what happens when we are triggered, where it comes from and how we can override unhealthy responses is a total game changer. Practices like mindfulness, meditation, and self-reflection help us develop a compassionate relationship with ourselves, providing the inner security needed to face life's challenges with resilience, harmony and flow.

2. **Connecting with others (interpersonal)**

I learned that fear is an emotion that naturally causes us to seek connection with another human being for comfort and support. When young children encounter something frightening while exploring their environment, they instinctively reach out to the closest trusted person. Toddlers are not ashamed of their fear. They long for connection.

Attachment is absolutely vital for us humans, who are a species of "dependent infants". In former times, if a baby were to lie alone 2 meters behind its caregiver by a campfire at night, it could all too easily be taken by a predator. The deep-rooted need for physical closeness in both the child and the mother is of existential importance. If this closeness is interrupted, it triggers a so-called attachment alarm in the brain and the autonomic nervous system switches to survival mode.

Unfortunately our culture has a tendency to judge and avoid feeling fear in general. Often a child's expressed fear is approached with a mental explanation why there is no reason for fear. We learn from an early age that we supposedly "don't need to be afraid" and that we better not be afraid. So we begin to suppress those feelings and hide them when with others. We would rather pretend that we are fine and avoid meeting others in times of emotional vulnerability.

Key insight

Open-heartedly sharing all aspects of being human fosters intimacy, which in turn forms the bedrock of trust, safety, and a sense of belonging.

Numerous scientific studies have highlighted the significant role of social connection in the integration and healing of trauma. Social interactions that involve trust and bonding can trigger the release of oxytocin, a hormone known to reduce stress and promote feelings of safety and well-being. This biochemical response can help mitigate the physiological impacts of trauma.

3. **Connecting with your Soul (transpersonal)**

   In the hustle and bustle of life, it's easy to forget that deep within us lies a force greater than any external circumstances – our Soul.

   The Soul can be seen as the innermost essence of a person, a deep and timeless aspect of one's being that is resilient, wise, and inherently knows the path to inner peace and unfolding of our potentials.

   Listening to one's Soul involves tuning into this deep inner voice and presence, which often communicates through intuition, inner knowing, and a sense of resonance with certain paths or decisions. This process requires a quieting of the mind, a deepening of presence, and an openness to what arises from within.

   Key insight

   A deep connection to our Soul provides a sense of purpose and belonging that transcends our immediate circumstances. This transpersonal connection can be nurtured through spending time in nature, meditation or other spiritual practices. It helps us tap into a profound sense of peace and trust in the greater flow of life, offering a sanctuary from the uncertainties and fears of the external world.

Exploring and embracing my inner world, open heartedly connecting with others and listening to my intuition has become my new compass through life.

Forged By Pain And Shame

"What the caterpillar calls the end of the world, the master calls a butterfly."

— LaoTze

The early 2000s had been vibrant and fulfilling—happily married, raising a wonderful son, living in an alternative community that mirrored my values. My work as a Transpersonal Life Coach and Couples Counselor felt aligned with my passion for healing and growth.

Then, on a cold December afternoon in 2010, just before Christmas, my world shattered. My husband and I went for a walk, the air heavy with unspoken tension. After a deep breath, he finally spoke: "I can't find my own strength and direction next to you anymore. The feeling of always falling short, of never being enough, has worn me down over the years, and I just don't have the energy to keep trying."

His words shattered my heart in ways that hardly allowed me to continue walking. Tears streamed down my face. Beyond my own panic at the thought of losing him, I could sense the deep pain he had carried for so long. In that moment, I felt a wave of desperation, realizing he was searching for something I simply couldn't give.

After nearly 20 years together, my husband, the man I thought I would grow old with, told me he was leaving.

This situation blindsided me. It was as though someone had ripped out my heart, leaving me hollow and lost.

Though our marriage had its challenges, I believed we could continue overcoming them together, just as we had done repeatedly over the past 20 years.

Just two months later, he told me he had met someone new, a woman with whom he felt stronger and more at ease, he said. That revelation broke me. I spiraled into a nervous breakdown. I couldn't function. I wandered aimlessly around our apartment, now empty of him, unable to shake the dagger lodged in my heart. The thought of him loving someone else was unbearable. I couldn't eat, couldn't sleep, and the smallest thing would bring me to tears.

I had always helped others through their crises, but now it was my turn. The pain went deeper than I could have ever anticipated. Professionally, I also felt shattered. How could I guide others in their relationships when my own had fallen apart? I felt like a fraud. The work I once loved felt unbearable, and I began to doubt everything—my beliefs about love, my role as a therapist, and even my own self-worth.

Thankfully, I had a community that became my lifeline. Friends would sit with me, hold me, and let me cry. One couple was just about to start a house project for people in times of crisis, and though it wasn't officially open yet, they took me in. Each morning, I would crawl into bed with my friend, needing to be held by her just to make it through another day. I felt like a fragile bird that had fallen out of its nest, utterly lost.

There were moments when I secretly wished my husband had passed away instead—not because I wished him harm, but because then I could have held onto the love and the belief that we would have grown old together. Instead, facing the reality that he had chosen someone else made me painfully question everything—my worth, my purpose, and my work.

In some of those dark moments the loving Universe surprised me with its magic. Time and time again, when I felt lost and overwhelmed, existence would send a sign, a person, or a moment of grace that lifted me up. It was as if I was gently reminded that I was not alone, that love and support were always present, even in the most unexpected ways. These moments of magic, when I needed them most, filled me with awe and deep gratitude for the invisible forces that carried me through.

One day, as I was rushing to catch a train, I suddenly broke down, sobbing uncontrollably. In my head, I kept asking, "How long will this pain last?" Out of nowhere, I heard my name. I looked up and saw my dear friend Shambala, who had gone through a similar heartbreak years earlier. The incredible part? She didn't even live in Germany—she lived in Spain and had spontaneously decided to visit her sick mother in Germany. It felt like more than a coincidence, as if the universe had sent her to me at exactly the right moment. She hugged me tight and whispered, "It will pass, sweetheart. It takes time, but it will get better." In that moment, it truly felt like an angel had appeared to remind me the universe had my back.

Despite those magical, uplifting moments, there were days when I couldn't hold onto that light—days when the weight of pain and shame made me want to disappear. So, I took a year off from my career to fully dedicate myself to transforming this life-altering upheaval into a journey of growth.

Mapping a New Path

"Life isn't about waiting for the storm to pass, it's about learning to dance in the rain."

— Vivian Greene

Slowly, my self-judging thoughts proved to be unfounded. The reality was that this chapter of my life led me to profound growth and transformation that no seminar or training could have ever facilitated. The heartbreak that once crushed me eventually became the catalyst for an even deeper understanding of myself. With the unwavering support of both professionals and friends, I was able to turn this challenging situation into an intentional journey of transformation.

At some point I was able to reframe the whole situation and no longer think that the divorce was a failure—it was a profound spiritual journey, and my Soul had chosen this path for a reason. I promised myself that I wouldn't let this heartbreak harden me. Instead, I used it to open my heart wider, to confront the depths of abandonment and insecurity within myself while deepening my confidence and self-love. That became my guiding light through the darkness.

Although I couldn't see it at the time, losing my marriage and questioning everything I thought I knew, ultimately allowed me to rebuild my life in even deeper alignment with my Soul.

Resilience building Milestones

Here are just some of the key skills I gained through this intense journey, which I invite you to reflect on:

Grounding and Centering: I became adept at grounding myself, enabling me to find calm and centeredness even in the face of scary uncertainty and frightening emotional pain.

How would your life change if you could find inner stability no matter what challenges arise?

Self-Love and Acceptance: Embracing myself fully, I let go of perfectionism and released the weight of shame and guilt. Self-love became my foundation.

What would it feel like to accept yourself lovingly and let go of self-criticism?

Inviting Intimacy: I transformed my relationships by shifting from control and demands to a softer, more inviting approach. This created deeper, more authentic connections that were free from blame and filled with mutual trust.

How much more nourishing could your connections be if you felt free to show up as your authentic self?

Mindset and Manifestation: By understanding the impact of my thoughts, emotions, and beliefs, I realised the importance of cultivating a mindset aligned with the life I desire. This allows me to manifest my deepest aspirations and transform my external world.

What if changing your mindset could lead to the life you desire?

Intuition and Inner Guidance: Instead of being trapped in cycles of overthinking and self-doubt, I learned to trust my inner voice. This connection to my intuition brought clarity and confidence to my decisions.

What if following your intuition brings a sense of ease and flow to your life, even in the face of uncertainty?

Developing The Harmony-MAP for my Dream Life

These invaluable skills and insights have not only helped me navigate my own challenges with greater ease but have also enriched my ability to guide and support others on their journeys. Drawing from my core learnings I developed a highly effective mentoring program called ***Harmony-MAP.*** This *MAP* is a powerful transformative **M**indset **A**lignment **P**rocess that integrates neuroscience, transpersonal psychology, and timeless spiritual wisdom.

Embodying this alignment allowed me to create a new life that reflects my heart's desires. Finally, I brought my dream to life by leaving behind the long, dreary German winters and relocating to the sun-soaked shores of La Palma in the Canary Islands. Now, with the beach just steps away, every day feels like a vacation, where the warmth and ocean breeze remind me that I'm living the life I once only imagined.

Life has also brought me great blessings in love. The man I now share my life with is a much better match on so many levels. While my ex-husband will always hold a place in my heart, I am profoundly grateful for his courageous decision to end our marriage. It allowed us both to find partners who are truly more aligned with who we are.

Uprooted by a Volcano, Anchored in My Soul

On September 19, 2021, the sun was shining brightly, and the day seemed peaceful. I had just bought some vibrant hibiscus plants for my patio, and by 3:00 p.m. I had finished repotting them, proudly snapping a picture of my newly refreshed outdoor space. Moments later, a loud rumble shattered the calm. Turning around, I saw a towering column of grey smoke rising ominously behind the house.

The air was filled with a sharp, hissing sound, like an enormous Bunsen burner. The volcano warnings for the island La Palma that I had stubbornly brushed aside had become a terrifying reality—the volcano had erupted, just 1 kilometer behind our home.

Panic set in as I quickly gathered my most essential belongings and joined the stream of cars fleeing the danger. This was the start of yet another long, agonising phase of uncertainty that stretched on for weeks.

Evacuated on the neighboring island, I watched as the lava crept steadily, day by day, closer to our home. For an entire month, I lived in a state of nerve-wracking uncertainty, checking daily updates, holding on to a fragile hope that our home might be spared. But with each passing day, more land was swallowed until, finally, the inevitable happened – our home was lost. The loss wasn't sudden – It was a slow-motion disaster, unfolding over weeks as my inner state shifted between hope, fear, and moments of acceptance grounded in deep trust in my Soul's guidance.

For weeks after the eruption, I woke up each morning with a deep undercurrent of fear coursing through my body, a persistent reminder of the trauma still lodged in my nervous system.

"Will you return to La Palma? Stay on La Gomera? Go back to Germany?" Friends kept asking, but I had no answers. I simply didn't know. I had to stay open, trusting my intuition step by step, without any clear plan, just faith in the process.

But despite the lingering uncertainty, I turned to the Harmony-MAP tools that had become my lifeline. These practices became my anchor during this period of upheaval. Applying these tools, I managed to ground myself, calm the inner turmoil, and listen to my Soul's guidance. Slowly, I regained stability.

One day, I felt a strong urge to visit La Palma. As soon as I arrived, I felt "home." While chatting with a friend, I mentioned wanting an apartment in a particular village. She advised me to forget it - so many people who had lost their homes to the volcano had already settled there, and finding an apartment in that village was next to impossible. Yet, I followed my gut. A casual coffee outing led to a serendipitous meeting with German friends who had just purchased an apartment in that exact village and offered to rent it to me. It was so beautiful, with a terrace and a breathtaking sea view.

This moment felt like pure magic, a testament to the power of trusting and following my intuition. I hadn't given a second thought to worst-case scenarios or obstacles, and as a result, I found myself living in this dreamlike space, all because I followed my Soul's guidance.

Experiencing a volcanic eruption - such an unpredictable force of nature - showed me vividly that we have no control over external circumstances. However, it left a deep impression on me that our inner attitude toward life itself plays a crucial role in finding peace of mind and shaping our lives. Trusting in the guidance of our Soul has proven to be the most solid foundation for true resilience. This insight inspired me to name this approach the "Soul-Based Resilience Mindset."

Diamond Insight

The most profound insight from my life story is that fear-driven attempts to control life lead to tension, contraction, and disconnection from our inner wisdom. Clinging to certainty and predictable outcomes blocks the natural flow of life and creates suffering by keeping us in constant vigilance against inevitable change.

The key to true harmony and resilience lies in finding the balance between holding a clear intention and surrendering to how the universe delivers the outcome. It's essential to have a vision deeply anchored in alignment with our Soul's essence but equally important to stay open to how life unfolds. This approach allows us to tap into a greater flow of creativity and ease.

The real treasure is mastering the ability to remain C.O.O.L. - **C**entered, **O**pen-minded, **O**pen-hearted, and **L**istening - in the face of uncertainty. By doing so, we can hear the whispers of our Soul, guiding us step by step toward a life aligned with our deepest truth.

Get your own Harmony - MAP

This entire experience of the volcanic disaster was not only a test of my personal resilience but also a profound validation of the Harmony-MAP program. This journey solidified my belief that Harmony-MAP can lead anyone through life's most unpredictable upheavals. It is designed to help individuals and couples to regain stability in the face of uncertainty, strengthen their connections with loved ones during times of upheaval, and create a new life they love in alignment with their Soul's essence.

Facing a major life change or just seeking deeper Soul-Alignment?

Access my free resources, including guided meditation, workbook and video inspiration scan the QR code.

ABOUT THE AUTHOR

ESTHER HEESE

SCAN TO KNOW MORE

Esther Heese is a Resilience Mindset Mentor and Conscious Relating Expert with over 30 years of professional experience. Trained in Transpersonal Psychotherapy, Integral Couples Therapy and Mindfulness, Esther has guided hundreds of clients worldwide through life-altering upheavals. Her mentoring seamlessly blends her expertise in depth psychology with an integrated focus on the spiritual dimension of being human.

Shaped by her own challenges, she embodies and imparts a profound resilience, rooted in deep Soul- Alignment.

Esther supports individuals and couples through high-level 1:1 and group mentoring programs, offered online in both German and English.

START OVER VOL 1

CHAPTER

9

"The Fallen Cellist:

Reforged By Fire, Darkness, and Ancient Stone"

JEROME ZORAN

If I could go back in time and speak to my younger self, I would look him in the eyes and say, "Jerome, no matter what darkness you face, you have the power to transmute that pain into spiritual gold. Never underestimate the quantum power of your mind and voice. You were born for this."

Halstead, Braintree, Essex is where my story begins. My early life was steeped in a unique blend of agricultural labor and the arts.

My parents were deeply connected to the land, and their lives were a symphony of tilling the earth and making music. Family friends often recounted that during my mother's pregnancy, they could feel an almost tangible, musical energy surrounding her as she worked on the fields.

It was as if the rhythm of life itself was already pulsing through me before I entered the world. Our family at that time was part of a larger community, and we were all builders of something new—something that bridged the old ways of living with a more conscious, spiritual path.

My parents played in a band, composing, performing, and living their music, while simultaneously engaging in the hard work of agriculture.

But it wasn't just music and farming that wove through our lives; a deep spiritual calling was the undercurrent that guided us. When I was just a year old, that calling took us to Glastonbury, a place known for its mystical energy and spiritual significance.

My parents felt drawn there as part of their spiritual evolution, and it became the backdrop for much of my early childhood. The first seven years of my life were marked by the complexities of adult relationships and the familial tensions that often arise in close-knit communities. My family, along with other relatives and friends, fostered a large, like-minded community centered around sustainable living.

They were pioneers in the vegan movement, creating innovative, cruelty-free meals long before plant-based diets became mainstream. And to this day, we are fond of healthy eating. Food and music have always been connected in our family. At the age of six, I began learning the cello, an instrument that would become my voice when words failed me.

My connection to music was innate, almost as though it had always been there, waiting for me to pick it up and play. Our home was filled with crystals—living symbols of the spiritual energy that permeated our lives.

From as early as three or four years old, I was captivated by these stones.

I would play with them, feel their energy, and watch as my father lovingly polished them with eucalyptus oil.

One day, curiosity got the better of me, and I drank some of the oil. What followed was a traumatic episode of poisoning that significantly affected my breathing for a little while after.

A few years later I had suffered some recurring throat issues, and now feel that these were symbolic—was there something I was struggling to express, something in my voice that was blocked, that I had no words for at the time?

Amidst these physical challenges, I also experienced emotional turbulence. My mother, deeply sensitive in her own right, was often weighed down by her own sorrow.

Her relationship with my father, once bound by the joy of music, began to unravel.

The dissolution of their band and their growing emotional distance culminated in their separation when I was just seven years old. This was the third major upheaval in my young life, and it left me feeling a tad lost, and disconnected from that loving family energy.

The years that followed were filled with emotional ups and downs for me. Melancholy became a constant companion, although looking back, I didn't exactly know that that was what I was feeling...

...not just for me but for my mother as well.

Even as a child, I could sense her deep sadness. I later learned that my mothers grief stemmed not only from her separation from my father but also from the tragic loss of her first husband, who had taken his own life when she was in her twenties. This loss had left an indelible mark on her, and though I didn't fully understand it at the time, I instinctively tried to lift her spirits with my presence and positivity, saying "everything's going to be alright mum, I'm here."

School was another battleground.

I was frequently bullied, though I could never quite understand why. I often found myself alone, which didn't bother me at first, but as the bullying escalated to physical violence, it became unbearable.

In one particularly brutal incident, where a boy choked me against a fence, and held me there for what seemed like an age, I could not breathe . After this incident, and after many discussions with my mother and the school, the decision was made to homeschool me when I turned eleven.

Despite the emotional and physical challenges, music remained my sanctuary. I continued to play the cello, and when I joined a local youth orchestra, I eventually became the lead Cellist, having ten Cellists to lead. Music became more than just a hobby—it was a lifeline, a channel for the emotions I couldn't articulate.

Around this time, I also became more attuned to the spiritual practices in my home.

I had learned that as a result of her healing herself from her wounds, she had herself become a professional healer, and a widely known spiritual teacher, working with and channeling her spirit guide, 'Ascended Master Chung Fu'. I often witnessed people from all over the world coming to her for healing sessions and spiritual guidance. When I turned 17, I had my first spiritual session with my own spirit guides, guided by Ascended Master Chung Fu (my mothers spirit guide) and other highly evolved ascended beings from the Elven realms and the Pleiades Star system. It was then that I began to understand that my sensitivities were gifts, not burdens.

Ascended Master Chung Fu said I had worked with him in many lifetimes and that he recognised me and told me I had unique abilities with sound, particularly in the realm of clairaudience, which is a psychic gift, enabling me to hear beings from higher dimensions, and even other celestial realms, Mozart was one known to have this magical ability to hear the Celestial Spheres…

With my gifts I hear the knowledge of my personal spirit guides and receive divine power through their frequency. Well as you might guess this opened up a new world for me, changing my life in miraculous ways. But suddenly life threw me unexpectedly into the deep end of a bottomless pit of darkness…

2009. The year everything fell apart. It wasn't a slow, creeping darkness, but a sudden, brutal shock. One minute I was washing dishes, the rhythm of soapy water, strangely comforting after a nice family walk. The next, a deafening crash. As I turned round to place a Pyrex bowl on the side, It shattered into shards exploding in my left hand…

The pain was instant, searing, shocking. It wasn't just pain; it was a violent intrusion, a brutal violation of my perfect hand. I looked down, a wave of nausea washing over me. My finger… was hanging off my hand. It hung there, a limp, bloody mess. Shock crept in deeper as I fully registered that the glass had cut through all my nerves, tendons, arteries, and pulley tendons.

I felt a feeling of terror growing from within me bigger than a mountain of shock, blood spraying everywhere, I felt another deeper level of panic set in, I had never felt this kind of energy before, my confused state, I found it hard to believe it was all happening. There was just too much blood leaving my hand, I felt paralysed, only just hearing my sister in law say "Jerome, wrap this clean T Towel around your hand, quickly now..."

In that single, horrific moment, I knew my carefully and joyously constructed future had slipped away—the life I'd meticulously built around music—sunk through hard... like quick sand. The years of practice, the hours of dedication, the soaring melodies and heart-melting harmonies I'd poured into my cello, all seemed to evaporate and disappear through a vast void, a gaping portal that just opened up in my hand. My identity, woven like a giant spider web into the music that I became, was torn apart.

It wasn't just a finger; it was the leading power of my whole musical life... the feeling of terror grew, it was a new terror of an unknown I could feel leading to a deep terribly dark realm... All I could hear in my head was... 'would this be the total loss of a part of myself, would I be able to save this finger? Would I make it back into the light... The feeling of not knowing was an immediate feeling of doom, a feeling of darkness I knew I would never escape.

The silence that followed was deafening. My audio field was obliterated, replaced by a terrifying void, there was no music in this feeling. A cold dread settled over me even deeper. It wasn't just physical pain; it was the soul-crushing weight of a stolen future. The deeper darkness that descended wasn't gradual; it was a suffocating blanket, smothering the last flickering embers of hope. Despair, raw and unyielding, twisted into a knot of terror in my stomach. My grief was a tidal wave, threatening to drag me under and drown me in its depths..

My family rushed me to Yeovil hospital 45 minutes away, and I felt that a part of my soul had vacated. As I sat in the car clutching my left hand wrapped in a blood soaked towel I had no capacity to accept my fate, I felt very confused.

When I got to the hospital, they said, "I am very sorry, but it's Boxing Day, there are no Specialist Doctors here, they're all on holiday". The words hit like a ton of bricks followed by a lightning bolt of cold hard sweat, as I felt my consciousness fall into a dark pit of fear.

"We can apply some butterfly stitches, and then you will have to drive to another hospital" I heard. I thought maybe this was a joke, but no, they meant every word.

We hurried to the next hospital in Bristol, and yes, you guessed it, no hand specialists there either. They said the best we can do is send you home and call you when the Doctors return from Holiday. The anxiety creeping in hit like a hundred hammer blows to my reality.

The drive home was darker than the deepest mountain. Getting back home was the very strangest feeling, every part of me expecting to be in an operating theatre. I lay in bed watching time pass by. Every day I would reignite my agony to change the bandage, and on the third day, I was hit with more shock, as I noticed half my finger had turned black. I dropped into deep prayer mode, calling and calling to every heavenly Being I knew the name of. Please don't take my finger. The blood throbbing, the pain growing and growing, I could feel electric currents, striking down my finger, but not following through. This was pain like I had never experienced before. By the fifth day, my whole left finger on the underside had turned black.

My thoughts turned black too.

Then I got the call, I was to go into Bristol immediately to be seen. The best hand specialist Doctor of the southwest of England was back from Holiday and was informed of my serious situation. Heading in again was a vastly different experience dosed up on painkillers, completely numb, I felt white cold sweats with a deep feeling that the whole world was Alien to me. I was taken straight away to be seen after waiting 5 days, the seriousness of the situation was frightening, would they take my finger off? Would I ever play music again?

Going into the operating theatre, they said "if we're going to try and save your finger, we will need to give a full general anaesthetic, I nodded.

I woke up hearing voices. It was the hand Doctor. I was struggling to hear what he was saying as I felt I had been travelling through space and time. Finally i heard him say, "your very lucky, we nearly could not save your finger, we had to reach deep into your hand to pull the tendon back up, you're very lucky"

I said thank you Doctor, and began to cry.

The nurse came next and said "drink this, you have been out cold, 8 hours 45 minutes."

The days that followed were a blur of pain, fear, and uncertainty. The feeling of vulnerability was too much to admit. I felt weak. The pain from before was nothing compared to this, with my whole arm, hand and finger now strapped to my chest, tight inside a huge brace, I felt trapped in a prison of pain.

Every visit from the nurse came with a serious warning saying, "Be very careful, any sudden movements and the tendons could rip apart, keep your arm and hand as still as you can for the next 48 hours." Now I knew this was a test of letting go, I just needed to feel and allow the journey to unfold, and let go more until my hot salty stinging tears fell in torrents like waterfalls of their own…

Even though I was tanked up on morphine to dull the sharp ripping pain like thunder bolts of white hot electricity, there were still moments when I felt completely hopeless, and helpless, trapped in a suffocating darkness that seemed to stretch out endlessly, offering no path to escape.

I was on a ward with many other serious cases, but this didn't seem to make me feel any increase of compassion for my situation. I just wanted to forget now, forget the vibrant colours of my life before—the joyous colour of my life, the rich hues of the cello's varnish… I was angry, falling into victim thinking.

And yes I wanted to be back in the lush loving greens of the fields surrounding my childhood home, the warm glow of shared laughter—but then it all faded again, just a fleeting feeling… slipping away into a monochromatic landscape of despair. I couldn't see a way out inside this dark realm of pain, no glimmer of light to guide me through the oppressive gloom. I felt utterly and completely lost.

But even at my lowest, the universe hadn't given up on me.

In the depths of this despair, I sought solace in meditation. It was during one of these sessions, while immersed in deep stillness, that a faint whisper, a glimmer of a voice, pierced the darkness. The message was subtle, almost imperceptible—a quiet urging, an intuition rather than a clear command: *"go on a hunt for a healing tool"*. The voice offered no specifics; no direction, just an undeniable sense of purpose. I didn't know what this tool would be, where I'd find it, or even exactly what it would do. But the whisper, soft yet insistent, ignited a spark of hope in the overwhelming darkness. It was a call to action, a nudge towards a path I didn't yet understand but felt compelled to follow.

Following the whisper's guidance, I felt a strong pull to seek external help. I went into town, a quiet determination driving me forward, and found myself drawn to the local crystal shop. Stepping inside, I approached the woman behind the counter, a feeling of urgency within me. "I need the most powerful tool you have," I said, my voice trembling slightly, "to heal pain." She paused for a moment, and then replied, "Let me look in the crystal bible real quick..."

Skimming through to find stones and crystal tools to heal pain, and boom, she found THE stone that fit this mighty purpose. She said softly, follow me, I think I've found it. The gravity of her words resonated with me and I imagined as though she had struck a vast vine of gold in a deep mountain of unknown riches.

She led me to a back room and we sifted through many crystals, and then there it was, the dark powerful shimmering ancient Shungite stone. It pulsed with a quiet strength straight into me, and I knew right away I had just touched base with an ancient force. A source of energy that was primordial. As I held the stone, I could sense the bright light inside it, the weight of its energy, the palpable sense of its history, and how strange that it seemed to hardly weigh anything, and black as midnight, but with a silver shimmer running through it like fragments of star light. The woman opened the "crystal bible again" – and began to read about Shungite's many healing properties, from its ability to absorb negative energy to its capacity for promoting deep physical and emotional healing, and that it had unique molecules inside it called Fullerenes.

These were not just ANY kind of random molecule, they had cosmic quantum healing power. The sun's energy, poured into, and divinely stored within for 2 Eons… 2 Billion years to be precise. This condensed black sun, a potent power source compressed by the ages, lay waiting to be rediscovered. It was as if this ancient stone, packed with Fullerene power was meant just for me, a beacon of hope in my overwhelming darkness. I clung to the Shungite like a drowning man clutches a lifeboat, I didn't let it go and knew I was taking it home with me.

I began incorporating it into my spiritual practices, using it to ground myself and heal the deep wounds that had been carved into my soul. I slept with it, I woke with it, I read all I could find about it, and the more I read the more it blew my mind. This was indeed a mighty gift from a far away galaxy. I learned that its known origin was the planet Jupiter. Splitting off an asteroid belt from Jupiter and eventually bursting through space like a burning Star crashing into earth some 2 Billion years ago.

The Shungite was a vast power guiding me, but it wasn't just the Shungite stone that saved me. It was the practices I had learned growing up—the sacred toning, the chakra spinning, the fire ceremonies to cut ties with past traumas. These tools became my divine light weapons in the battle to reclaim my life.

Day after day, I fought. I worked with Shungite, spinning my chakras, chanting sacred sounds that vibrated through my very cells. I performed fire ceremonies, releasing the pain and trauma that had held me captive for so long. It wasn't easy.

There were days when the darkness threatened to swallow me whole, but I refused to give in. Every time I wanted to quit, I forced myself to take one more step, to chant one more note, to spin one more chakra.

And then, one day, something miraculous happened.

The Fight

During a deep meditation with my Shungite crystals, I heard the voice of my higher self whisper within me:

"Jerome, your wounds are your greatest gifts. Your pain has sculpted you into a vessel for divine light. Use your voice to heal, to inspire, and to awaken others."

At that moment, I understood. I had been forged in the fires of adversity. My pain was not my enemy—it was my teacher.

The realisation was not instant, nor was it gentle. It came like a slow, dawning light breaking through the dense, suffocating fog that had surrounded me for so long. For years, I had resisted my pain, fought it, and cursed it. I saw it as a thief, an intruder that had stolen my joy, my dreams, and my sense of self. But as I sat there in deep meditation, holding the Shungite stone in my hands, I felt a shift. It was as if the very energy I had spent so long rejecting had begun to reveal itself for what it truly was—not a punishment, but a gift.

I had been looking at my pain through the wrong lens. I had seen it as something external, something hostile, something to conquer or escape. But now, I realised that my pain was not separate from me—it was a part of me, an integral thread in the tapestry of my soul's journey. It was not something to fear or resent but something to embrace, to explore, and to transform.

I began to understand that pain was not the opposite of joy, but its counterpart. One could not exist without the other. Pain was the shadow… the BLACK GOLD that gave depth and dimension to the light. It was the contrast that allowed me to fully appreciate the beauty and richness of life. Without the deep valleys of sorrow, the peaks of joy would lose their meaning. My pain has taught me resilience, compassion, and a profound understanding of the human experience. It had broken me open, forcing me to look at the parts of myself I had long ignored or buried. And in doing so, it has given me the opportunity to heal, to grow, and to evolve.

I realised that this was the essence of alchemy—not the literal transformation of lead into gold, but the spiritual transmutation of our heaviest burdens into our greatest strengths, I call this our 'Black Gold'. My pain, which I had once seen as a weight dragging me down, was now revealed to be the very foundation upon which I could build a new life. It was the raw material of my transformation, the fuel for my awakening.

In that moment, I also understood that my pain was not mine alone. It was a universal experience, a thread that connected me to every other soul on this planet. Each of us carries wounds, scars, and shadows, and it is through these shared struggles that we find our common humanity. My journey through pain was not just about my own healing—it was about learning how to guide others through their own darkness, to help them see the light within their shadows.

I began to see my pain as a sacred teacher, one that had come into my life for a reason. It had stripped me of everything I thought I knew about myself, leaving me raw and vulnerable, but also open and ready to receive a higher truth. And so, at that moment, I made a choice. I chose to stop running from my pain and instead to face it head-on. I realised that I was not a victim of my circumstances. I was an alchemist, a Crystal Sacred Sound Shaman, a Shungite Warrior of the Soul. My pain was not the end of my story—it was the beginning of a new chapter, one in which I would rise, transformed and empowered, to live my true Higher Self purpose.

This was the turning point, the pivotal moment when I saw clearly that every challenge I had faced, every wound I had carried, had been leading me to this realisation. My pain was not my enemy—it was my greatest teacher, my most profound gift, and the key to unlocking the infinite power of my soul.

From that moment on, I knew my mission. I began to channel high-frequency healing music, creating guided meditations and leading sacred sound ceremonies. I realised that my voice—my true instrument—was more powerful than I had ever imagined. It wasn't about the cello. It was about the sound within me. Through my work with Shungite and the teachings of Ascended Master Chung Fu, I discovered the quantum power of the mind and voice. I learned to alchemise pain into spiritual gold and manifest my deepest desires into reality.

I had learned that true leadership comes from within, from a place of peaceful power. I developed online programs and digital wellness products, helping others heal and awaken to their own power. I became a guide, a mentor, and a leader now working with and alongside Chung Fu—guiding not by force, but by the power of humble grace and joy. And now, I stand here as living proof that you can rise from the ashes of your greatest challenges and become unstoppable.

If I could go back and advise my younger self, I would tell him, "Trust in the journey, even when it seems impossible. The darkness is just a part of the process. You were born to rise."

The Shungite Warrior: Mastering the Alchemy of Pain and Power

The Shungite Warrior Training hadn't been an easy journey. Every step I took, every breath I inhaled, brought me face-to-face with the darkest parts of myself—my doubts, my fears, my grief.

But as I dug deeper, I began to understand that this darkness held something precious. It wasn't a void to be feared.

I discovered I could access Ancient Teachings from Ascended Beings as I spiritually trained with my Shungite crystals. These Ascended teachers revealed to me a new language, a way of describing this deep stuff that is hard to identify, and which I have named as the 'Black Gold'. This is the shadow within us, the neglected and wounded parts of our soul. It was the 'Black Gold' deep within—the dense, powerful, transformative energy that could be harnessed, purified, and turned into spiritual light.

It is the unresolved emotional pain and mental anguish that we carry, often without realising it.

But in the sacred work of the path of the Shungite Warrior, crafted from excavations of my own soul, spanning over 20 years we learn that this pain is not to be avoided; it is to be embraced, transmuted, and made sacred.

The first step in this alchemical process is understanding the nature of pain. Pain, whether mental, emotional, or physical, is energy.

It is dense, heavy, and often stagnant. But in the presence of Shungite, this energy begins to shift. Shungite, known for its powerful grounding and purifying properties, acts as a conduit between the denser frequencies of pain and the higher frequencies of divine light.

When used in conjunction with sacred sound, this process becomes even more potent.

In my training, I was taught to perform a practice I now call 'Shungite Sacred Sound Golden Shadow Work'. It is a combination of Shungite's grounding energy, deep meditation, and the use of sacred sound to activate and transmute the shadow—the 'Black Gold'—within us.

This practice is rooted in the belief that 'sound is the primal creative force of the universe', and when directed with intention, it can break up stagnant energy and dissolve the illusions of pain, allowing us to reclaim our power.

The Process of Shungite Sacred Sound Golden Shadow Work

The practice begins by entering a deep state of stillness, holding a piece of Shungite in hand, and allowing its energy to ground you. Take a moment with me now…

Close your eyes and visualise the 'Black Gold'—the dense, heavy energy of pain or emotional trauma—within your body. See it as a dark, shimmering substance, heavy yet powerful. Allow yourself to feel the weight of this energy without judgement or resistance. This is the first step—'acceptance'.

Once the energy is fully perceived, begin to tone a sacred sound, one that resonates deep within your soul. The sound can be as simple as an "Om" or a personal mantra that connects you to your higher self. As you make this sound, visualise the 'Black Gold' beginning to vibrate and shift, breaking up into particles of light.

The Shungite in your hand amplifies this process, pulling the dense energy down into the Earth, where it is transmuted into light. As you continue to tone, feel the

'Black Gold' dissolve. What was once heavy and stagnant is now fluid, 'golden light', pulsing with the energy of creation. This is the alchemical process—the transmutation of pain into spiritual power.

With each tone, you are not just releasing pain; you are 'transforming' it into creative potential, into the energy that will manifest your deepest desires. At the core, what crystals really help you do, is manifest. Crystals and sound are at the heart of everything. This is the essence of the Shungite Warrior—to turn pain into power, to turn darkness into light, to turn 'Black Gold' into divine manifestation.

This is where my life went up notch, and I began to study the vast esoteric world of manifestation, bringing forward this knowledge in my one to one sessions.

Manifesting with Sound

Sound is the primal force of creation. "In the beginning was the Word, and the Word was with God, and the Word was God." The Word, the sound, is the creative principle that brings into being all that exists.

Sound is vibration, and vibration is the essence of all matter. When you make sound, you are engaging with the very fabric of creation. You are speaking your reality into existence.

When you speak your desires out loud, you are aligning your inner vision with the external world. The vibration of your words transforms the energy of your thoughts into physical reality.

It is not enough to simply think about abundance; you must declare it, affirm it, and embody it. As you speak your truth, you are sending out ripples of energy into the Universe, and the Universe responds.

Let us consider the power of the "I AM" statements. When you say, "I am abundant," "I am prosperous," or "I am love," you are not merely making a wish; you are declaring a truth.

The words "I AM" are the most powerful words you can speak because they align you with the divine essence of creation.

The sound of your voice, combined with the power of your intention, creates a powerful vortex of energy that draws to you the things you seek.

Crystals: The Keys to Discovering Your Divine Potential

Crystals are not just beautiful objects; they are living beings, vibrating with the energy of the Earth and the Cosmos.

They are the physical embodiment of the crystalline matrix that underlies all of creation. When you work with crystals, you are tapping into a deep well of ancient wisdom and power. You are connecting with the Earth herself and with the divine intelligence that governs the Universe.

For example, 'Shungite' is a powerful grounding stone that connects you to the Earth's energy, while 'Citrine' or Libyan Gold Tektite are known for their ability to attract wealth and prosperity.

Crystals are the physical embodiment of the crystalline matrix that underlies all of creation, holding within them the vibrational memory of the Earth and Cosmos. They are tools of transformation, helping us tune into higher frequencies of healing, intuition, and abundance. For example, **Clear Quartz** amplifies energy and intentions, while **Amethyst** enhances spiritual clarity and protection. **Rose Quartz** radiates unconditional love, and **Black Tourmaline** shields against negativity, grounding you into the Earth's energy. Each crystal serves as a bridge, connecting us to the ancient wisdom of the Universe.

When you work with crystals, you are forming a partnership with their unique energy fields to amplify your intentions and catalyze transformation. These powerful allies can enhance meditation, healing, and manifestation practices, helping you align your mind, body, and soul with your highest potential. By working intentionally with crystals, you awaken to their guidance, unlocking pathways to your divine purpose.

The Power Lies Within You

My friend, you are a powerful being of light, and you are here to manifest abundance in every area of your life. The tools of sound, crystals, and the guidance of the Ascended Masters we work with are here to assist you on your journey. But ultimately, the power lies within you.

You are the creator of your reality, and you have the power to shape your life in any way you choose. The Universe is abundant, and that abundance is available to you right now. All you need to do is align with it, to claim it as your own, and to step into the flow of divine creation.

May you walk in the light of abundance, beloved. May you manifest all that your heart desires, and may you know the joy and freedom that comes from living in alignment with your divine truth. Blessings upon you, now and always.

From Darkness To Destiny - Rise With Shungite Power

Beloved soul, the time has come. You've felt it stirring within you—the call to rise, to step into your full power, and to manifest the divine purpose you were born to live. The universe is waiting for you to claim your place as a creator, a healer, and a light in this world.

No longer do you need to carry the weight of your past, the pain, or the limitation that has held you back. You are ready to transform all that lies in the way of your greatness. You've always known that you were meant for more, and now is the time to act on that knowing.

I invite you to join me on this profound journey of transformation.

Scan the QR Code to begin your journey toward manifesting your highest potential, with the Quantum Voice Activation Tool Kit.

Blessings and Love Jerome Zoran

ABOUT THE AUTHOR

JEROME ZORAN

SCAN TO KNOW MORE

Jerome Zoran, known as the Shungite Guy in Glastonbury UK, has been dedicated to serving mankind as a transformational energy coach, showing you ancient ways to access the hidden realms of your being. Through the potent alchemical power of Shungite crystals and the multi-dimensional healing energy of sacred sound you see how easy it is to unlock your deep golden wellspring of abundance and unstoppable joy, and its all YOURS waiting to be claimed. With Jerome Zoran you can step beyond the limitations of your current reality and manifest a life of extraordinary purpose and fulfillment. Walk with Jerome and rediscover your 'Black Gold', the true power of your Soul.

CHAPTER 10

"Kicked, Beaten, and Left Behind:

Turning My Chaos Into Triumph"

RYAN TADJOU

I was born amidst chaos—literally. In 1992, in Blida, a town nestled in the foothills of Algeria's snowy Atlantic mountains, serenity was a far cry from the reality surrounding us. My mother recalls how, during the Algerian Civil War, extremist terrorists and the liberal government fought over who would rule the country, bringing death and destruction in their wake. My arrival into this world came under the shadow of conflict, born during a war.

Even a routine prenatal check-up for my mother was dangerous, as getting her to the clinic safely meant navigating back alleys and side streets. My father, wearing a beard that could signal allegiance to Islamists, had to sneak her through parts of the city to avoid the random violence. I was smuggled into this world.

Nights with my mother were punctuated by the sounds of gunfire and the faint whispers of fighters handing out food and ammunition outside our window before they'd vanish into the Atlas Mountains to ambush morning patrols. I was named Ryan Tadjou, though my parents gave me another name, one I've since abandoned. Those early years taught me lessons in fear, with extremism and survival woven into the fabric of our days.

My earliest memories are of a household where religion was rigidly enforced, more like a prison than a sanctuary. My father, a devout man who had studied in Saudi Arabia, decided that, as the civil war intensified, we would be safer if we left Algeria. We abandoned our home to the extremists, who quickly repurposed it as a food storage facility for their cause. We left, but it wasn't long before the conflict reached our family again. Not long after our move, my grandfather back in Algeria was arrested. Not for any crime, but simply because he prayed. The government classified him as an extremist and detained him in a desert camp for eight months. Faith came at a high cost.

Saudi Arabia brought us out of one danger and into another. It was safer, but that safety came with shackles. We moved from Riyadh to Jeddah to Makkah, chasing my father's work opportunities, but no matter where we went, life felt restrictive. I had a sister a year older than me and later a brother, and together, we felt the weight of control. When we finally returned to Algeria after the war, true peace was elusive. Though extremists had surrendered their weapons, corruption still simmered in the background, and so did my father's authority. He'd shut the windows when neighbors held weddings, claiming that music was "haram" and a threat to our purity. Yet I'd lie with a small radio under my pillow, listening to Algerian Rai music, feeling the first pangs of rebellion.

And then, a darker shadow fell over my early years, one I've struggled with for decades. When I was six, maybe seven, or eight—honestly, I've blocked much of it from memory—I was molested by a worker at my grandfather's factory.

My mind, for years, buried this trauma, but the reality is, it happened. The man lived in one of the extra rooms at my grandfather's estate, a setup common in our family's practice of hosting workers who stayed for months on end. We shared food, and as an extroverted child, I mingled with everyone. Somehow, I was drawn to smoking back then, perhaps as an unconscious way to rebel. When I asked that worker for a cigarette, he struck a deal with me—a deal I couldn't understand, one that exploited my innocence.

In exchange for teaching me to smoke, he took advantage of me. The trauma settled deep, surfacing only recently in therapy, and even writing about it now reawakens a knot in my gut. It's a memory that never truly fades, hiding under layers of years, waiting to sting whenever I draw close. It's left scars I still carry, scars I didn't fully realize until much later, like a live grenade inside me.

My need for independence didn't stop at music or the forbidden cigarette. By the time I was ten or eleven, I was already dipping my toes into business. My first venture? Selling phones.

Nokia 3310s were all the rage, and though it wasn't much, it taught me the value of making my own money. I'd buy and sell phones between school and after-school classes, careful not to let my father notice, knowing he had no patience for anything that didn't fit his vision of me as the obedient, pious son.

One particular deal stood out. I'd traded up from a Nokia 3310 to a Sagem 5, then to a Sagem 7 with a camera and a privacy door in the back. The thrill of those small transactions felt like my own secret life, a life outside his grip. But one day, a disgruntled customer came to our house, complaining about a faulty phone. My father found out, and my little business came to an abrupt end. He shut it down without offering an alternative, but that experience had already lit a fire in me. I'd had a taste of control, of autonomy, and I wanted more.

Rebellion and Defiance: The Battle Begins

Though my father and the extreme religious environment at home suffocated me, a rebellious spark always burned inside. I grew up as the "second man" of the house, especially when my father was away, shouldering responsibilities far too young. I bore the brunt of his punishments as well. While I relished being "the man" in my father's eyes, the standards and punishments felt heavy, suffocating. Religion, once force-fed to me, transformed into rules I longed to break. Not out of disbelief, but because it felt like shackles.

My father's temper was infamous. He ruled our home like a dictator, punishing every misstep and enforcing rigid rules often loosely aligned with Islam. He'd beat my mother, and I would try to defend her, earning my share of bruises in the process. Once, he cracked my skull with a wooden stick, landing me in the hospital. He made me lie to the doctors, telling them I'd fought neighborhood kids to shield him from the consequences. Protecting the one who should have been my protector became my reality.

Isolation became a familiar feeling, even in a house full of siblings. My younger brother, ever the golden child, knew exactly how to stay in my father's favor. He'd snitch on me without remorse, watching as I faced the consequences alone, while I was the one defending him in the streets. He never bore the bruises or felt the sting of shame from a slap that lingered visibly on my face. By eleven or twelve, I began distancing myself from the family. I started to run, finding small ways to escape—even when it was only in spirit. One holiday, knowing a trip would be just another controlled extension of my father's strictness, I chose to run away. I managed to evade his car for over three kilometers before hiding in a graveyard, feeling a strange peace among the stillness.

My first real act of open defiance happened on that day. I wasn't just sneaking music or dabbling in small business ventures; I was rejecting the life he had built for me. That was the beginning of my fight for freedom.

The Birth of a Dream: Flying as Freedom

Dreams had little room to grow in my family, where ambitions were routinely crushed before they could take root. The idea of flying—of becoming a pilot—was the first real dream I clung to. I didn't even know what university was until high school, when classmates discussed their own futures. For me, the thought of flying was a symbol of escape—a way to rise above the constraints of my father's control, beyond rigid religious expectations, and away from the trauma I hadn't yet fully processed.

Flying meant freedom, distance, and seeing the world from a new perspective. But even this dream felt unreachable. My father had his plans for me, urging me toward Islamic Law. Despite excelling academically, I was funneled down a path that had nothing to do with my aspirations. He promised I'd get to choose my future if I succeeded in school, but by the time I graduated, he had sent me to an Islamic high school, where my fate seemed pre-determined, regardless of my achievements.

But that dream never died; it simmered beneath the surface, waiting for the right moment to ignite. I had tasted small freedoms through rebellion, yet the dream of flying burned quietly, patiently, as I continued through the motions, always hopeful that one day, I'd be able to reach it.

Crossing the Threshold: Early Attempts to Break Free

From a young age, I could feel the disconnect between my world and what I sensed could be possible. Without the words to express it, I felt it in my bones—a constant, quiet urge to escape. I lived under a roof where every choice was made for me, every action scrutinized, every mistake punished. So, I sought escape through small, quiet acts of rebellion. Rai music, banned in my household, became my lifeline. The lyrics whispered of freedom, joy, and individuality—everything my life wasn't allowed to contain. Lying under my pillow at night, I listened to the forbidden songs on a small radio, each note a taste of the world outside the rigid lines my father drew.

Looking back, it wasn't just music. It was the idea of having something that was mine in a life where control was absolute. That small defiance stoked the fire in me, and I wanted more.

Father's Influence: The Path I Didn't Want to Take

While I was busy rebelling quietly, my father had already mapped out my life, each piece of my future perfectly placed in his plan. To him, my path was clear: I would pursue Islamic studies, because, to him, that was the only respectable future. I would attend Islamic high school and earn a scholarship to the Islamic University of Madinah, fulfilling his own unfulfilled dreams. My future was already spoken for, according to him, and there was no room for deviation.

Inside, however, I rebelled. Quietly, secretly. I excelled in school, not to meet his expectations, but because I knew education could be my escape. My grades would be my leverage, my bargaining chip. And in the quietest parts of my mind, I held onto my real dream. The dream of becoming a pilot. Flying wasn't just a career aspiration; it was liberation. To lift off, to soar above everything that weighed me down—that was what I yearned for most. Every plane that flew overhead seemed to call to me, whispering of escape, of freedom, of leaving behind the life I knew.

Yet, I kept that dream to myself. My father would never understand; to him, flying was foolish, even sinful. His life plan was a road I didn't want to walk, but I went through the motions, studying hard and excelling, keeping my dreams hidden, but alive.

Meeting Kye was like finding a light in the darkness, a guide when I had almost forgotten that hope existed. People say that a mentor appears when you're ready, but I wasn't sure if I was ready or simply too broken to believe in anything. Yet Kye found me. We'd crossed paths before, but I had never imagined how crucial he would become in my life. Kye was seven years older, carrying a calm wisdom that felt foreign to me. In a life marred by chaos, his steady demeanor, his way of listening without judgement, and his belief in me were a revelation.

I remember the day he invited me to stay with him. At that time, I had nothing left to offer, but he extended his hand anyway. He didn't just provide shelter; he gave me something far more valuable—a place to breathe. That corner in his dorm was the first space I could call my own, where I didn't have to fight for survival or worry about who was watching. Kye didn't try to fix me; he simply showed me another way to be. He had a quiet resilience that made me believe in myself, not through any grand gesture but by offering the time and space for me to process my story.

Through Kye, I was introduced to a world beyond my own narrow survival. His home, Singapore, was unlike anything I had known, but he never belittled my ignorance. Instead, he opened doors for me, patiently showing me a bigger world, a new perspective, and the possibility of a life beyond mere survival. Seeing the Marina Bay Sands through his stories was like catching a glimpse of another planet, and with that, the seed of change was planted.

Kye didn't magically solve my problems, but he helped me understand that there was more to life than pain. He became my lifeline, the reason I found the strength to rebuild. With his support, I began to realize that my circumstances didn't define me; they were just chapters in a much longer story. Slowly, I rebuilt myself, not through any life-altering advice but through Kye's friendship, warmth, and open mind. He helped me discover a way forward, one where I was not just a survivor but someone with a future worth fighting for.

In time, I traveled with Kye to Singapore and, eventually, to Malaysia, expanding my vision of the world and seeing life beyond survival. Malaysia was a fresh start, a land free from the constraints of my past but fraught with its own challenges. Moving there felt like shedding an old skin and stepping into a new identity. I was no longer the boy hiding under his father's control or the man scraping by on the streets. Malaysia symbolized freedom, an opportunity to rebuild who I was from the ground up.

Enrolling in a Master's program felt like my first true declaration of independence. Specializing in Teaching Arabic to non-Arabs wasn't just about academia; it was a reclamation of my heritage on my own terms. This choice reflected a deep attempt to craft a path uniquely mine, free from the dictates of my father's plans. Education became my way to rewrite the narrative of control that had once ruled my life.

But life in Malaysia was more than just academics. It demanded survival in a new form. To support myself, I ventured into entrepreneurship—opportunities I'd never considered before, like acting, events management, and content production. These pursuits became avenues of reinvention, channels where I finally felt in control of my destiny. Every event I managed, every project I completed, felt like another piece of my story, a step further from my past and closer to the future I wanted.

Yet, even as I climbed, the shadows from my childhood followed me. My father's oppressive control, the trauma I had endured—none of it vanished just because I changed my environment. The weight of those experiences crept into my personal life, affecting my relationships in ways I hadn't anticipated. I had managed to survive rock bottom, but the battle against the internal demons was far from over.

As I achieved outward success, I grappled with a darker part of myself. I struggled with infidelity, a painful reminder of the cycles I had vowed to break, the very behavior I despised in my father. It was easy to justify it, to pretend I was different, but deep down, I knew I was causing pain in a way that echoed the legacy I had tried to escape. The realization was crushing—despite my best efforts, a part of him lingered in me.

Balancing this personal turmoil with my career was exhausting. The outside world saw success: a man with a career, a family, and a future. But beneath that surface, I was haunted by the past. I was repeating patterns, struggling with the same secrecy, the same rebellion, the same conflicts. Every time I hurt someone I loved, I felt I was turning into the very person I had spent my life running from.

In that period, rebuilding took on a new meaning. It wasn't about professional achievements; it was about facing my darkest parts, acknowledging my flaws, and fighting the cycles that threatened to define me. Every day became a battle, a commitment to something better, to become more than just a product of my past. It was the hardest journey I had ever undertaken, but if there was one thing I had learned, it was that survival wasn't enough. I had to strive for something greater. And that's what kept me moving forward, even as I wrestled with my shadows.

Amidst this turmoil, an old dream resurfaced—the dream of becoming a pilot. As a child, flying had represented freedom, an escape from the life I was forced into. But over the years, that dream had been buried under survival, lost in the shuffle of overcoming one struggle after another. Now, with a new life in Malaysia, that dream felt within reach again, symbolizing not just a career goal but a final act of defiance, a reclamation of the freedom I had been denied.

Earning my Student Pilot License became a turning point, a victory over everything that had tried to keep me grounded.

I remember the first time I sat in the cockpit, my heart racing as I prepared for takeoff. That moment was more than just a career milestone; it was a declaration. Every fear, every trauma, every obstacle I had faced melted away as the plane lifted. For the first time, I felt truly free, untethered by the weight of my past, flying above the darkness that had tried to claim me.

Reflecting on that journey, I realized how far I had come. From the streets of Saudi Arabia, where survival meant washing clothes in public restrooms and sleeping on plastic bags, to the skies, where I finally felt in control. Every struggle, every misstep, every scar had brought me to this point. Flying wasn't just about breaking free; it was about honoring the boy who had dreamed of the sky while lying beneath a ceiling of limitations.

Achieving this dream wasn't just for me. It was proof that anyone who has faced adversity can rise. It was a message to everyone who had been told they were not enough, that they would never escape their past. I was living proof that persistence, resilience, and courage could defy even the darkest odds. For the first time, I was in control of my own story, soaring above everything that had once tried to keep me grounded.

My journey didn't end there. I realized that true growth lay in giving back, in becoming the very mentor I had once needed. As I found success professionally, people started to look to me for guidance. It felt strange at first, to be the one others turned to, but I saw in them the same confusion, the same hunger for hope that I had once carried. Mentoring became my new purpose, a way to offer others the light that had guided me.

Through mentoring, I realized the transformative power of my own journey. It was more than just survival; it was a path to empowerment, a way to help others find their own light. I called myself the lighthouse, a beacon for those lost at sea, offering a hand as Kye had once offered to me. Every story I heard, every person I helped, healed a part of me. It was a reminder that the darkest moments could fuel the brightest lights.

In the process, I confronted my shadows—not to banish them but to understand and embrace them. The trauma, the mistakes, the regrets—they were as much a part of me as the triumphs. I had spent years running from them, thinking they would disappear if I just moved fast enough. But I learned that the shadows are what make the light burn brighter. I had to face them, accept them, and use them as fuel for my growth.

Now, I stand here, not as a perfect version of myself but as someone who has learned to balance light and dark. I don't have all the answers, and I never will. Life isn't about perfection; it's about learning, evolving, and finding peace amidst the struggle. I've found my way, and now I'm here to help others find theirs.

Looking forward, I see myself as a beacon—a lighthouse guiding others through their storms. My vision for the future is a place where people, regardless of their past, can find guidance and clarity. I want to create a community, a space where people can come for hope, for light, for direction. The journey hasn't ended; it's just evolved. Together, we rise, not despite the shadows but because we have learned to embrace them, to transform them into something greater.

This is the legacy I want to leave behind: that no matter how dark it gets, there is always a way forward if you keep your light shining. I am Ryan, the lighthouse, and my light is only just beginning to rise.

If you want to connect with Ryan you can scan the QR code.

ABOUT THE AUTHOR

RYAN TADJOU

SCAN TO KNOW MORE

Ryan Tadjou, is a visionary marketing and technology professional with over seven years of experience in marketing strategy, events management, and cutting-edge fields like AI and Web3. Known as "The Web3 Man," Ryan specialises in blending innovation with strategy to empower businesses in navigating the complexities of the digital landscape. As Managing Director of Annaba Resources, he led international projects with seven-figure budgets, integrating AI and blockchain solutions to drive success. At KCOM Academy, he revolutionised marketing and event strategies, incorporating NFT technologies and digital transformation tools. Ryan also founded Hungry Apes Club, merging blockchain with F&B, showcasing his ability to pioneer Web3 applications. Certified in AI for Business, his expertise spans AI-driven content creation, predictive analytics, and blockchain consulting. Whether leading multimillion-dollar campaigns or training AI systems, Ryan thrives on transforming ideas into impactful realities, redefining industries, and inspiring growth.

CHAPTER 11

'Beyond the Brink:

♥ *A Journey of the Heart Through Illness, Loss, a Life Reclaimed and New Beginnings'*

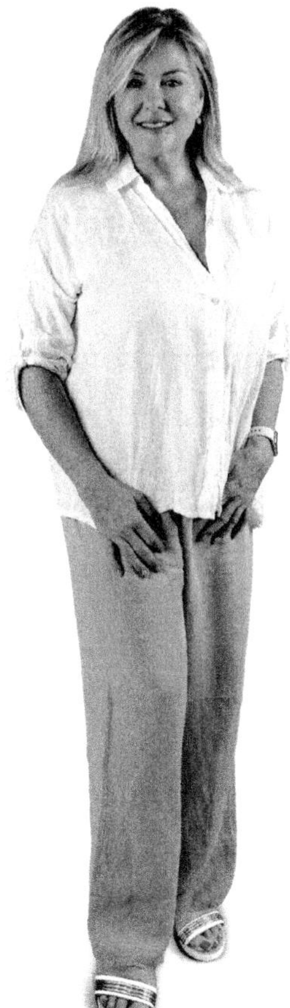

JULIET McCANN

A gripping tale of resilience, courage and the indomitable human spirit that will inspire you to chase your wildest dreams and never give up on yourself.

DISCLAIMER

This chapter is a reflection of my personal experiences, thoughts, and emotions. While it draws upon real events, it is presented from my perspective and should not be taken as a definitive account of the events or individuals involved.

To respect the privacy of others, no names or identifying details have been included. Any resemblance to actual persons, living or deceased, is purely coincidental. This work is intended to share my journey and insights, not to assign blame or pass judgment.

The warm September evening promised fun with friends, but as I rushed to get ready, my heart began its familiar, frantic dance. "Oh no, not again," I thought to myself, trying to shake off yet another palpitation attack, hoping that my heart would return to its normal rhythm.

Much later the following day, my heart still pounding, I managed to get a doctor's appointment, my vision blurring as I struggled to explain. The doctor's response to the ECG was one of panic. "We need to get you to the hospital. Now!"

The world became a whirlwind of flashing lights, the ambulance siren and frantic voices. I had seen enough medical dramas and caught onto the terminology to know that this wasn't looking good!

The medics rushed me into the ER. My heart was a ticking time bomb in my chest. My whole world blurred as I asked myself

"Is this it? Is this what it looks like to stare death in the face?"

At just 16, my life flashed before my eyes as they prepared to restart my heart.

I looked up into the eyes of a nurse who was caressing my hand.... What if this was the last face I would see?

"Please," I whispered, "I'm not ready to go." She reassured me that everything would be ok....

Everything was a blur... I don't remember if I was awake or not. I just recall that the defibrillator's jolt hit me like lightning and everything went black...

The next thing I remembered was opening my eyes...what a relief! ...I'm awake, I'm alive!

I was rigged up to drips and monitors galore and had doctors and nurses buzzing around.

Later the doctors came back in to see me together with my father.

"You're lucky to be alive. It's a miracle that you didn't collapse as your heart had been pacing at well over 300 beats per minute for more than 24 hours." the doctors told me.

My father's face was grey with worry, his eyes welled with tears. As he held my hand he whispered "We almost lost you". I felt sick to my stomach to think that I had put him through such an ordeal. I'd been given a 2nd chance and I vowed I would go on to live my best life and make him proud!

I was transferred to a specialist hospital where I underwent countless tests for the next couple of weeks. I was finally diagnosed with a rare heart condition, one which was very unusual for a person of my age. I became a medical curiosity, my condition became one of the key case studies for the medical students there. I was just glad that something good had come out of this. I was also secretly proud to think that I was somewhat famous, albeit only in this medical school!

In the years to follow I was plagued with further life threatening attacks leading to hospital dashes and defibrillator episodes. Medications became my lifeline. Some years later, I became one of the first and the youngest patients in the country to undergo correcting this condition with a cardiac ablation.

As I emerged from the haze of anesthesia, a surge of emotions washed over me - relief, gratitude and an overwhelming sense of possibility. My heart, once a ticking time bomb, now beat with renewed purpose. This wasn't just a new lease on life - it was a rebirth. The world lay before me, a canvas of infinite possibilities, all of which I was going to embrace with open arms. I vowed that I would value every moment moving forward and go on to live a life of purpose!

Fast forward several years...

I moved overseas to start a new job, leaving behind everything familiar to me, apart from my deep-rooted insecurities of course, stemming from my childhood, they had a habit of following me wherever I went!

My mother's alcoholism resulted in her spending much of my childhood years in and out of specialist clinics and hospitals. By the age of 6 she was no longer living with us and all that was left were painful memories and an overwhelming fear of abandonment. My amazing father became both parents, determined to give me the best life possible.

In my later life and in order to compensate for my insecurities, I'd throw myself into my work and true to form, here I was again, burying myself in my new role, all work and little play apart from the odd evening out with colleagues.

This one evening I met a guy. He was a bit older than me and I found myself drawn to him. He lavished me with attention and compliments very early on. We ended up in a relationship and as time went on, my guard was down and now I was all in! I had to learn to put my trust in someone someday right? I mean what's the worst that could happen?

One evening I went over to his house. He'd recently given me a key which I'd never used. He wanted me to just come over whenever I wanted. He was out this one evening and I thought I'd surprise him and be there when he got home. He loved surprises. His car was there in the garage so he was already home.

I rang the doorbell, there was no answer. I tried to call his phone and there was no answer. Now I was worried. What if something had happened to him? What if he had collapsed? I quickly let myself in. The house was dark downstairs so I made my way upstairs. My heart started to race as I began to think of the different frightening scenarios. I reached the landing and could see a light on in the bedroom. As I approached the door I heard some muffling sounds and what sounded like a door closing. What on earth was happening? My heart began to race. I entered the bedroom and he was in the bed. He said that he had got home earlier, was tired and hadn't heard my calls. Something didn't seem right. He said that I should go home and he would call me the next day. This wasn't like him. He would normally be so happy to see me, tired or not. As I turned around to leave, I noticed that the photo of us both which was normally on the desk was not there. This was strange. I then noticed a light under the crack of the bathroom door. Suddenly my heart started to beat faster and faster... was there someone else here? I went over to open the door and it was locked. Someone was in there.

"What's going on?" I asked, my voice trembling. "Who's in there?"

He began to fluster and started shouting at me that I was just imagining things.

"I am not stupid, tell me what's going on. I am not leaving until you tell me."

With that he jumped out of the bed and got dressed. He refused to explain anything and instead he ran out of the house and I just heard the screech of his car speeding away. Meanwhile, I was left standing outside the bathroom door. I could hear heavy breathing.

"Please come out," I said. "I just need to speak with you."

I sank to the floor with my back against the door. My head was pulsating and my hands were shaking. I honestly didn't know what I was going to be faced with or how I would handle it. I just wanted answers. After some time, I heard some movement behind the door, the door was being unlocked, I stood up and watched the door handle slowly turn. My heart was pounding.... As the door opened I saw a young woman before me, her nakedness wrapped in a bath towel. She pushed past me and was searching for her clothes which had been hurriedly tossed under the bed. She started dressing frantically and was ready to run!

My heart was beating so hard I felt as though it was about to burst out of my chest. I had my biggest fears beating down on me, crushing me down to the ground. This was the man who I had allowed into my heart and who I had put all of my trust into. At that moment, the whole situation felt unreal. You see this kind of thing in the movies... It doesn't happen in real life. I stood there and literally felt the blood running from my veins. I was in complete shock. I felt like I wanted to just scream and run but my body wouldn't move. It was like I was frozen in time. The only thing moving was my heart which was beating so hard from the adrenalin...

I couldn't even look at her but I did want answers...

"Who are you and how long has this been going on?"

"Do you know about me? Did you know that he is in a relationship?"

I asked the questions so matter of factly as if I was conducting an interview... I didn't even know if I wanted the answers to these questions. I was totally numb. I felt physically sick.

"It's not what it looks like." the woman replies... Seriously? What a bloody cliche!!!

All of a sudden I have this surge of inner strength, fuelled by adrenaline and anger...

"Not what it looks like? I'll tell you what it looks like… it looks like I've just walked in on you and my boyfriend in bed together… that's what it bloody well looks like. Now tell me if I am missing something here?"

"If you want answers you should speak to him." She spurts...

"Well if you hadn't noticed, your lover has gone running and fled the scene leaving YOU to face the music SO I am asking YOU for answers! After what I have just walked in on, I think you owe me that, don't you?"

It turns out that this has been going on for several months and she knew about me… blah blah blah… the rest of it just seemed to blur into insignificance. She gathered her things, abruptly brushed past me, ran out of the house and fled into the night.

Before I left, I found a piece of paper lying in the study. I wrote a note and left it together with the key simply saying "You screwed up BIG TIME! It's over!!! I'll bet you're glad you gave me that house key now aren't you?"

The aftermath was a whirlwind of pain and confusion. My heart, already scarred from childhood trauma, now felt shattered beyond repair. After a few months, I let him back into my life, too weak to fight and too scared to be alone. As time went on, his impatience with my healing only deepened my wounds. "Just get over it," he'd snap, as if flipping a switch could erase the betrayal. I walked on eggshells, terrified he'd leave if I showed my true feelings. But inside, I was screaming. I needed to get myself some help.

The weight of betrayal crushed me. I went for counselling to try and heal my heart which was shattered. My partner told me that this was my fault as he felt that I didn't love him enough and he needed more. What? I asked myself. He had ALL of me… there was nothing left of me to give!

I'd lie awake at night, wondering how I'd ended up here. What had happened to the promises I made to my 16 year old self who was given that second chance? I owed it to her to live my best life and this was anything but that. The strong, independent woman I once was seemed like a distant memory. At work, I was the picture of success. donning my mask of happiness and as I drove home, dread consumed me. Our home, once a sanctuary, now bore the scars of his fury - on the walls, on the doors and on my skin.

My mother wasn't well. She was suffering terrifying flashbacks and panic attacks from a fall into the water a few weeks earlier.

"I just can't shake this feeling," she confessed one night on a call. I could hear the fear in her voice.

"Mum, please," I begged, "You need help. Real help."

"I promise I'll go back to see the doctor if I don't feel better in a couple of days." We agreed to speak again then.

A few days later, it's early evening and I receive a phone call. The news hit me like a thunderbolt…

"Your mother... she's passed away," the voice on the phone said. My world shattered in an instant. I fell to the floor, my heart breaking into a million pieces.

"What? How?" I asked. I could barely get the words out of my mouth.

The truth was even more devastating than I could have imagined. She had taken her own life. The guilt crashed over me in waves.

"Why didn't I call her earlier? I could have saved her!"

Childhood memories flooded back - broken promises, disappearances and the constant refrain: My father's ultimatum still echoed: "It's the drink or us." She chose the drink. She left me then and lived a life of regret over the choice she made and now this, she's left me again. Why would she do this? I felt guilty for having these thoughts and tried to banish them from my mind but the pain was excruciating and I was looking for answers.

The cause of death was not shared with others as it would have been too much for them to bear. I was numb as I sat and listened to how she had laid out all of her affairs in envelopes along the floor, in front of where she took her final breath. Everything was meticulously organized, right down to her final wishes, her funeral, which she had paid for together with her grave plot etc.

This wasn't just some random decision, it had been planned. Why didn't I see the signs? This is something which tortured me during the days, weeks and months to follow. There were many nights when I would fall asleep, just out of sheer fatigue from the heartache and tears which seemed to be endless. I didn't want to wake up. I longed to join my mother so that she wasn't alone. I felt isolated, trying to comprehend what had happened and why. I couldn't talk to anyone about it as I had made a pact. A promise which now felt like shackles.

"I'm so sorry mum." I would say over and over in my head. My mother had developed health issues and told me a few years earlier that if she ever became incapacitated, she planned to take the Dignitas route. I was the only one she had told this to. I refused to listen as it was too painful to think about and I told her that it would never come to that. I'd know if she would ever get to that stage.

"Why didn't I see the signs that she wanted to end her life?" I asked myself.

"Why didn't she leave a letter? She was always writing letters." These unanswered questions were killing me.

Desperate for answers, I threw money at mediums, hoping to connect with her. Grief consumed me, a dark journey I couldn't escape. My partner's initial support crumbled into anger.

"You need to get over this!" he snapped, his patience wearing thin. Grieving time for my mother meant less attention on him. This would lead to days on end of him ignoring me until he felt that I had sufficiently apologised for failing to attend to his needs. The narcissistic behaviour became increasingly controlling, suffocating me. I felt utterly alone, struggling to survive each day.

I hardly had time to grieve my mother's passing when my father fell sick and passed away. I was devastated. With my father, my protector now gone, it was like my partner knew that I was at my most vulnerable.

"You need me now more than ever," he said. This wasn't his way of offering me love and support… far from it. This meant that things were about to get a whole lot worse.

My work was my only escape but even there, I couldn't find peace. My partner's jealousy of my success festered like an open wound. "A woman should know her place," he'd say, his eyes blazing with contempt. "And it's not in some fancy office."

What a stark contrast this was... a career woman by day, forced into silence and submission by night. My partner's lack of ambition in his own job seemed to fuel his need to control and diminish my achievements. His angry phone calls demanding my immediate return home became a dreaded part of my routine and yet another battle I had neither the energy nor desire to fight.

In the depths of my despair, my dreams and aspirations became my lifeline. I would often find solace in scouring online images of the rolling hills of Tuscany, a place my father had painted so beautifully with his words. I had made a promise to him to follow in his footsteps and I saved countless images of the stunning Tuscan landscapes and quaint houses surrounded by sunflowers, my father's favourite flower.

My phone became my private sanctuary full of dreams which I put out to the universe to one day become my reality. In my darkest moments, I would lose myself in these pictures, my heart longing to be there and to be free. This gave me hope beyond the life I was living.

My heart raced as my partner snatched my phone one evening, his eyes narrowing at the images. "Why do you have these saved?" he demanded.

"It's my dream," I replied nervously. "To have a small house there one day, just like those in the photos..."

His face contorted with rage.

"You're just a bloody dreamer! Life isn't that simple." He sneered, hurling my phone across the room. It landed with a sickening thud.

I flinched, feeling another piece of my soul chip away.

The Final Straw

It was the early hours of the morning and I was woken by the sound of the doorbell ringing and fists pounding on the front door. We had both been out separately with friends. I'd arrived home hours earlier. Confusion washed over me, it was him. Why had he not let himself in? The spare key was in its usual place. As I opened the door, he lunged at me in a terrifying drunken rage "You locked me out!" he roared. Before I could respond, he grabbed me by the throat and thrust me up against the wall while he continued to roar in my face. He grabbed my wrists, dragging me and throwing me out into the night, locking the door behind him and leaving me out on the street. I had begged him to stop. He was a lot bigger than me so I had no chance of fighting against that kind of body strength. I was terrified. Barely dressed, out on the street, I knocked desperately, begging to be let in.

Eventually he unlocked the door. I rushed inside, only to be met with a cold command: "Get out. Go to a hotel. I don't want you here!" On a number of occasions after previous violent outbursts, I had gone to stay in a hotel in a bid to seek refuge from his behaviour. This cycle of violence, apologies, and reconciliation had become a grotesque dance, one I could no longer bear to perform. This was the final straw. He had gone too far. My safety had once again been compromised. There was no end to what this man would do to me.

As dawn broke, I woke up and felt an unexpected wave of confidence and inner strength. I left the house and drove around the surrounding neighbourhoods, looking for a place to live. I felt a mix of fear and hope. Years of suppressing my true self, of walking on eggshells, had taken their toll. I knew that this was the right decision, the ONLY decision and yet even with that, I felt like I'd failed. This was the Catholic guilt kicking in!

Within a few days I had secured a rental contract on a place nearby to close friends who were aware of my situation. I'd known them a lifetime and their words hit me like a ton of bricks.

"It's been killing us to watch you fade away throughout this toxic relationship and we've been powerless to help."

I'd never even considered how my situation affected those around me who loved me and who had to bear witness to this.

Over time the facade began to crumble. The once-charming exterior of this man I was with, carefully crafted to win hearts and minds, started to crack and peel away like old paint. Slowly but surely, the true nature of the man emerged, a stark contrast to the illusion he had so meticulously maintained. As a result, friends I'd known forever, were distancing themselves. The thought was devastating and that familiar ache of abandonment started creeping in.

It was the day of the move and my friend arrived to help me, determination etched on her face. "Come on," she said, extending her hand. "Let's get you moved into your new home!" I felt lost and overwhelmed by the finality of it all. This home which we had moved into together, once brimming with dreams, now echoed with the ghosts of a failed relationship. How does one pack up a life? How does one box memories, both bitter and sweet?

I suddenly broke down. My friend came and sat beside me. The tears were rolling down my face as I looked around the room at all of the things which we gathered over the years, every item carrying a memory. I was deeply saddened that the relationship had broken down and was irreparable. I'd made relentless efforts over the years to fix things... and to fix his anger issues and in the process I'd compromised myself, my health and wellbeing.

"I don't think that I can do it, I can't leave... not today, I'm just not ready…"

My friend asked me "Why don't you feel ready?"

I replied, "I was the one who found this place for us and I love it, this has been my home and now I am having to leave it. I feel really sad."

She paused for a moment and then went on to say...

"Oh yeah, you've had some great times here... just look around you." She goes on to point out the marks on the walls and the broken, patched up wall accessories which became many of the casualties of my partner's angry outbursts.

Then she says...

"Just remember one thing, we've had to live through this terrible ordeal with you so if you do decide to stay then go ahead, get on with it, put up with it and shut up about it!"

I took a double take… trying to look at her through my teary eyes… this was tough love indeed but couldn't she see how difficult this was for me?

She went on to say…

"Look at you now, despite all of the pain and the suffering, you still look good, you've got a great job and are an attractive woman. Now let me ask you a question…"

"Let's say that you decide to stay… then let's fast forward 5 years from now... you're another 5 years older. Can you picture what your life looks like then? Are you happy?"

At that precise moment, I felt like something had struck me with full force… It was almost like I'd been brought back to life with a 1000 volt charge from a defibrillator. Much like my 16 year old self, I was being jolted into reality. I owed it to her to take action. I wasn't going to let her down this time.

As I pictured that future life, I literally couldn't breathe, it looked terrifying! I suddenly pulled myself together, stood up and said "No, no, no… I need to get out of this NOW!"

I looked over and saw a footstool next to my friend which I had bought a few months earlier and as I wiped away my tears I said "I bought that and I really like it… it's coming with me."

My friend jumped up and rubbed her hands and said "Right, she's back! We're back in business! Now let's get packing!"

In the months and years that followed, I embarked on a gradual process of healing through hypnosis and other methods. I began the arduous task of rebuilding my shattered self. I was broken, damaged but not beyond repair.

I started my new life in a beautiful house which was way too big for me and as part of my healing I had to love myself and do whatever would bring me joy. I had Post It notes stuck to doors, walls and mirrors all over the house with affirmations of self love and how much I was loved and worthy of living the best life ever!

For the first time in years I was sleeping soundly without the fear of the terrifying rampages which used to vibrate throughout my home and to my very core.

I'd invited a few close girlfriends over to celebrate my new home and new found freedom. As they read all of the self love affirmations, they raised a glass and said…

"Well look at you… in this fine big house, all for yourself... you're certainly loving yourself now!!!"

Where is She Now? The Comeback!

In the years to follow, I went on to become who I am today... a happy, strong and successful woman.

I moved to a new country where I have enjoyed the most amazing career in real estate. I went on to win several coveted awards within the company and became the first female VP in a male dominated company and headed up the largest department within the organization.

I have grabbed life by the horns and gone on to do things I never would have considered possible in my previous life. I left the company where I had been working for several years. I had achieved what I wanted to and made it to the top of the corporate ladder which wasn't easy as a woman in what is still very much a man's world.

Life after the corporate world has been nothing short of incredible!! I'm in the process of writing about these new adventures and what is possible and what I've achieved.

I enrolled in an interior design course which was something completely alien to me! I knew that this would enhance my new property business so I grabbed the opportunity with both hands!

As well as researching and sourcing investment and lifestyle properties for my clients, I've also designed and developed turnkey villa projects from A-Z and gone on to create successful and profitable Airbnb businesses for them, achieving the prestigious Superhost status. This is a great way to generate a healthy passive income and create financial security for the future. I know all too well that there IS life after loss and independent financial freedom is key!

What an exciting journey this has been so far and you can see more about this here...

I have a dog who I absolutely adore!! I wasn't 'allowed' one in my previous life! My baby boy is the love of my life... together with the man I was destined to meet. He's my soulmate and my closest friend in the world. I am truly blessed to have these 2 amazing guys in my life!

I will now be expanding my business into Italy where I love to spend much of my time and where my dog can come too. The Italians LOVE dogs and they are welcomed EVERYWHERE!!!

Remember the part in my story when I used to save images of quaint little houses surrounded by sunflowers in Tuscany and that I was told that I was "just a big bloody dreamer?" Last summer I stayed in the same house in Tuscany which I had saved among my photos!

Lessons Learned & Advice to Self and Others:

Some of the most valuable lessons I have learned come in the forms of understanding and acceptance. The more I have learned about alcoholism the more I understand that this is an illness which consumes and controls those it inflicts.

Thankfully my mother was able to fight back and was stronger than the hold it had over her. I am so very proud that, despite losing everything she loved and cared for, she reformed herself and rebuilt her life.

I accept that someone's decision to end their life is their own choice to make. Given the circumstances that many people are faced with at the time presents them with no other choice.

I was fortunate to have received help and guidance and also read some great books which are focused on this matter, all of which provided me with a deeper understanding and have brought me a lot of inner peace. As a result of this I have been able to go on and help many others who have found themselves in similar situations. Knowing that I was able to help others deal with their situations means that my own struggles were not in vain.

I've learned we must look deep within and remind ourselves of how strong we are and what we have already survived. Pain is only temporary and there IS a way out and there IS life after loss. There are always many more people out there who are less fortunate and who have suffered greater losses than ourselves. One thing which I find so rewarding now is to be able to recognize this and give back to others. I am very lucky to be part of organizations whereby I can help others who really need help and who have suffered great losses such as children who have lost their parents at such a young age.

Another lesson I've learned is that whilst playing out the whole 'Pollyanna' role and being eternally optimistic and positive can be a good thing in life, it can also mask the brutal reality. We need to trust our instincts and if it doesn't feel right, recognise that early on and remove ourselves from the situation.

It's important to apply the same values and principles in all aspects of our lives, starting with our personal lives first and foremost.

Despite everything that happens to us in life, we are fortunate in that we still have an opportunity to start again… every day is a different chapter. We are the authors of our own life and if we don't like the first part of our book we get to change the story and write a different ending,

One last note... We must remember who we truly are:

I was born a warrior… My name 'McCann' is Gaelic and literally means:

'A young warrior'.

The McCann family motto is 'Virtue Thrives Under Oppression'... Well doesn't that just say it all?

ABOUT THE AUTHOR

JULIET McCANN

SCAN TO KNOW MORE

Meet Juliet, a vibrant soul whose journey began in the heart of London's Mayfair, where her family's bar and restaurant played host to the stars of British cinema. Her innate wanderlust led her into the travel and media industry, where her love for storytelling found its perfect match at a leading national newspaper.

With an entrepreneurial spirit and passion for property, Juliet ventured overseas into real estate, launching a remarkable journey in corporate leadership. Known for her resilient "unstoppable" spirit - which earned her the title of Company Value Champion - she's proven that setbacks are merely setups for comebacks.

At 55, Juliet gracefully pivoted from the corporate world following an unexpected career shift. Now she divides her time between three inspiring locations: the modern luxury of Dubai, the rustic charm of Tuscany, and the spiritual serenity of Bali. Her days are filled with Interior Design studies, property development projects and holistic wellness practices - including Sound Healing and Meditation Therapy certifications she completed in Bali.

When not working on her various projects, you'll find her enjoying life's simple pleasures alongside her four-legged companion, Mr Bojangles.

Looking ahead to 2025, Juliet is embarking on an inspiring new project: "55 @ 55" - documenting 55 new experiences undertaken at age 55. Through this creative endeavor, she aims to inspire others facing similar life transitions, proving that sometimes the most beautiful chapters begin when we least expect them.

START OVER VOL 1

CHAPTER

12

Brain Damage -

A Rollercoaster Journey from Jail to Phd

DR BRODY MILLER

The Deep Quest For Belonging

I grew up in a small, rural country town in North Carolina. Think cows, tractors, and that "everybody knows everybody" vibe. I was the only Jewish kid in my elementary school in a place where everyone is either named Bubba or Earl. I stuck out like a sore thumb. Kids at school often would tell me I was going to hell for my beliefs. Charming, right? Like, "Hey little Brody, you're not only different, but you're also eternally damned." How's that for a childhood trauma starter pack?

Don't get me wrong—I had awesome parents, the kind who'd make you breakfast and teach you about farming life. But no matter how many hugs and "I love yous" I got, it didn't shake that feeling that I was always on the outside looking in. I remember searching for answers, staring out at the endless fields, wondering if I'd ever truly belong somewhere. But I never seemed to find the answer. My thirst to fit in only grew.

I craved acceptance like a thirsty man craves water.

Searching for a way, I found my calling through sports. Baseball, basketball, football—if it involved throwing, catching, or running away from things, I was in. On the field, I wasn't "the Jewish kid"; I was just another dude. It was the closest thing I had to feeling normal. I got to hide behind a helmet or a jersey, and man, did that feel good.

But then life threw me a curveball. I got cut from the high school basketball team, and bam—my "happy place" was gone. It was like a rug had been pulled from under my feet, and I was back to being the outsider, the one who didn't fit in.

My chest felt hollow, like something vital was ripped away from me. And let me tell you, teenage angst is a whole different level of existential crisis. So, what's a boy to do? Well, if you guessed "turn to drugs and alcohol," then congratulations, you're right! Drugs and booze became my new "happy place," which at that time felt like a golden ticket.

And wouldn't you know it, they started calling me "Millertime," combining my last name and the popular beer brand. Not exactly a superhero name, but hey, it was something.

Finally, I was being noticed, welcomed, and even celebrated. It felt like I'd finally found a place to belong, even if that place was at the bottom of a bottle.

The only problem was that no matter how much I tried, I was still the square peg trying to fit in a round hole. Deep down, I only grew more insecure. No matter how hard I tried, my reputation was still the chubby outcast who couldn't even get a prom date. There was always that gnawing feeling that even when people accepted me, they weren't seeing the real me—just the mask I wore.

What started as a weekend fling with drugs quickly spiraled into something far more insidious. It wasn't long before I was caught in the clutches of addiction. By the time I reached college, drugs and alcohol weren't just a part of my life—they were my life. Every day, I was partying. If there wasn't a party, we would make up a reason. Drinking, smoking, and taking drugs was the only thing I was consistent at. They consumed me like a wildfire, spreading through every aspect of my existence.

I eventually decided to start selling the stuff to keep my habit going and to foster the sense of belonging that I so desperately craved. It started with weed—good ol' marijuana—but quickly leveled up to pills and whatever else I could get my hands on. Spoiler alert: things didn't exactly go great. The fall came fast and hard.

I remember one fateful summer night when I set up a deal outside my apartment with a regular buyer. I climbed into the back seat of a four-seater Coupe Deville, my "friend" beside me along with two guys I had never met before. Immediately, something felt off. I felt a deep sense of vulnerability. I thought it would be just another small deal: half an ounce of weed for $200. No big deal, right? How wrong I was!

When I pulled out the bag, I suddenly found myself staring down the barrel of a snub-nosed Smith C Wesson revolver. "Give me your shit, bitch!" he barked, as he cocked back the hammer of the gun. Time seemed to warp; I could hear my heartbeat thundering in my ears. A cold, eerie thought gripped me: Is this how it all ends? It was as if my life was screaming at me to wake up, but I couldn't hear it. I was too numb to care.

My bad karma continued to catch up with me a few months later when I was arrested for felony possession of MDMA. My concerned parents insisted I drop out of college and move home immediately. Following that, I was bouncing in and out of drug rehabilitation programs for YEARS. I honestly couldn't win without losing! But hey, at least I wasn't out getting robbed and committing felonies, right? Looking back, I know my parents' decision saved my life, but at the time, it felt like the final nail in the coffin of my freedom.

The Viral Night That Forced Me to Face My Demons

And then, ladies and gentlemen, came the night that really changed my life. Around 11 years ago, I'm outside this nightclub, belligerently drunk. In my drunken stupor, I decided it was a good idea to pick a fight with a bouncer. Yes, seriously—a bouncer who, by the way, was three times my size (he could've eaten me for breakfast). Dude threw a vicious haymaker that knocked me out cold in the middle of the street. It was so hard, that I was out for 5 minutes plus, and I finally regained consciousness in the hospital. Not only did I get my lights punched out, but to add insult to injury, the whole incident was caught on camera and went viral on the internet. A local news station broadcasted the incident.

Yep, by the time it was all said and done, over 100,000 people had front-row seats to my one-way ticket to Pavement City. The shame and humiliation went beyond anything I'd ever felt. It wasn't just embarrassment; it was the feeling of having hit rock bottom in a way that everyone could witness.

That night outside the club marked rock bottom for me. I'd already lost my dignity in private, but now it felt like my shame was plastered for the world to see.

The worst part wasn't the concussion or even the humiliation of the viral video. It was the gut-wrenching realization that I had no one to blame but myself. All my running, my hiding, my countless attempts to numb the pain had finally caught up to me, and I was left exposed and broken. That's what addiction does: it tears you apart piece by piece until there's nothing left but an empty shell. I had become the guy everyone pitied, the cautionary tale, the face of "what not to do with your life."

In the weeks that followed, I barely left my room. The weight of failure felt suffocating, a constant reminder of all the years I had lost and the bridges I'd burned. All my old friends wanted absolutely nothing to do with me. My family—bless them—still loved me, but I could see the exhaustion in their eyes, the silent plea for me to change before it was too late. The hardest part was the mirror. Every morning, I looked at my own face and saw someone I no longer recognized, someone I didn't want to be.

One morning, as I lay in bed staring at the ceiling, something in me snapped. I realized that if I kept going down this path, my story would end in tragedy. For the first time, I felt a spark of determination, a glimmer of hope that maybe, just maybe, I could change my story.

So, I took a step, just one step. I got myself into a rehab program—but one I took seriously this time. It wasn't easy. Rehab was hard in its own way, forcing me to face demons I'd tried to outrun for years.

But I stuck with it. I started counseling, learning about myself in ways I never had before.

A Message My Brain Couldn't Ignore

Fast forward a year into my recovery, on a sunny day—birds chirping, skies clear, and bam! My body decides to pull a full-on grand mal seizure while I'm talking to my AA sponsor.

Thanks for making things interesting! I woke up in a hospital bed, with doctors surrounding me, and telling me that they found 2.5 cm cavernous malformation on my left frontal lobe. My brain was literally bleeding. Awesome, right?.

A few months later, I went under the knife, my brain cut open to remove the malformation in hopes of ending the seizures. But life wasn't done testing me. I cycled through medication after medication—Depakote, Keppra, antidepressants, antipsychotics, pain meds like gabapentin. The side effects were brutal, and a violent reaction to Keppra even landed me in a mental institution temporarily. On top of that, seizures continued. I was recycled down the washing machine of one doctor to the next, and back again. Each new doctor seemed to give me the same blank stares and empty reassurances.

Needless to say, my memory suffered quite drastically afterwards. After many recovery programs and a failed surgery attempt, things were not getting better. In fact, they were getting WORSE. Naturally, I asked the questions, "Why did this happen to me?" and "Am I developing Parkinson's or Dementia"? I was forgetting where to put the most basic yet most important things like my keys or my wallet.

The Ray of Light In The Darkness

However, in my darkest hour, I found a ray of light. I was introduced to the idea of neuroplasticity by Dr. Joe Dispenza. He spoke about how the brain could change, heal and adapt in response to my thoughts, emotions, decisions and experiences.

I escaped the victim mentality that I'd adopted after having doctors tell me that I would have to live with my "Broken" brain. But even though I was told by doctors that things would never be the same again or that I'd need to be on medication for the rest of my life, they were right about ONE thing. Things would never be the same again! In fact, spoiler alert they have gotten better than ever before! My life truly took a 360-degree turn. Success and abundance followed me in all areas of life.

I no longer accepted the label that I had to live my grim diagnosis. I was no longer a prisoner to my past. Determined to transform, I attended a weeklong, Dispenza retreat that forever changed my life. During a deep meditation on a gorgeous day on the beach of Cancun, I felt a profound sense of wholeness, peace and connection to the universe . I can only say it was the most unfamiliar yet familiar feeling I've ever experienced. A direct connection to source, God and the universe. I truly felt the connection to myself, everyone and everything around me. I felt as I became the beach, the sun, the seagulls, I became everything!

After the event, my life truly took a 360-degree turn. Success and abundance followed me in all areas of life. Understanding the power of thought and the mind, I made over $100,000 dollars in the crypto market in a very short amount of time. I was able to buy my dream car at the time, a brand-new black Honda Accord. My wife and I adopted our wonderful dog "Heart" and moved to Colorado Springs, Colorado, a place where I had always dreamed of moving.

But life came to test me again with its twists and turns. The COVID pandemic hit, and as every one single person on the planet knows, it was a very tough and fearful timeframe. Things continued to get more challenging. In the summer of 2021, my wife's mother's health took a rapid decline, and she had to rush to Argentina to be by her side. Her mom passed away soon after, which hit both of us deeply. I was heartbroken and relapsed because I couldn't take the pain. At first, a couple of drinks helped numb things, but before I knew it, my drinking spiraled.

Within only a week's time frame, I began drinking heavily, trying to escape the overwhelming grief. I decided to start the day drinking and then arrived at the night where I sabotaged myself drastically. It led to a blackout and a car crash that led to my third DUI. Sitting in the jail's waiting room, reality hit me hard. Facing time behind bars was a harsh wake-up call, and I felt the weight of more of my mistakes. I ended up turning myself in after my birthday, entering a new, unknown world.

It honestly felt, at the time, that I was trapped in a prison of the past and that no matter how hard I tried I couldn't escape it.

Jail was, unsurprisingly, a tough environment, but it wasn't all violence and danger as I'd feared. Amidst the difficult routines and less-than-pleasant meals, there was a sort of camaraderie that was built. Fellow inmates and I found humor in small things—joking about the "five-star" menu, getting through the endless hours, and trying to maintain our sanity. The correctional officers even joined in on the jokes.

The biggest battle wasn't really with the environment—it was within. Guilt, shame, and regret lingered, but I found a way to hold on. Each day brought me closer to a fresh start. After release, I faced seizures and strict probation requirements. Still, every challenge only solidified my determination to rebuild my life. Although the road wasn't easy, I began to understand that this was building my character. Ironically, jail was not my low point.

Because I already had lots of knowledge and self-improvement tools, it became a situation where I could build up my mental and emotional resilience. Looking back, I see how trauma can trap us, but I also realize how gratitude, a bit of hope, and daily action can set us free. I maintained my good habits and made the very best out of my situation. In jail, I learned that I need to take full responsibility and accountability for my life because that realization will free me. I learned that you should never run away from your past because it will eventually catch up to you. It is part of you, which means that it is you. Instead, you need to learn to forgive yourself, let go, and make peace with it.

The Strength to Rise Again

The profound experiences I went through during and after my incarceration ignited a transformative journey that rippled through every aspect of my life. In the year that followed my release, I felt an undeniable shift not just within me but also in the world around me. I discovered the healing power of holotropic breathing, which can release the "spirit chemical" DMT (Dimethyltryptamine) in small amounts. DMT gets released when we are in a sleep cycle and creates the vivid lucid dreams we have. Techniques like this are a big reason why I have been able to let go of the traumas of my past and now feel better than ever before. After my release, in one of my deep visualizations, I had a remarkable moment that encapsulated my newfound sense of freedom. I envisioned a bald eagle leaping off a tree limb and soaring into the sky. In that instant, I felt an overwhelming rush of joy that resonated through every one of my 37 trillion cells. It was a profound realization of liberation and the potential for growth, symbolizing my journey from darkness into light.

This experience of connecting with my spirit animal infused my life with a vibrant sense of purpose.

Soon after, the universe connected me to my courageous and heartfelt mentor, Sir Marco Robinson. He guided me. He gave me powerful, tested, and proven strategies. My online business, which I had once seen as a struggle, began to flourish. The growth was not just in numbers but in the authenticity and purpose that underpinned every interaction and every piece of content I created. I found myself at peace like never before. I was no longer defined by my past mistakes or the labels that had once clung to me. Instead, I embraced self-love and gratitude every day. This new mindset propelled me to connect with and support those who had endured similar struggles, particularly concussion survivors and even world-class athletes who wanted to maximize their brain health. Among them was a world champion famous Boxer Dedicated boxer with a heart of gold. His humility and willingness to trust me in our work together not only inspired me but also reflected the resilience and determination that I admired.

Working alongside him allowed me to share my insights into recovery and mental resilience, while my commitment to helping hundreds of concussion survivors became a driving force in my life.

Recently our company's social media presence has exploded, Our account @drbrodymiller, gained over 200,000 followers on Instagram alone. Each new follower represented a connection, an opportunity to share knowledge, hope, and the power of resilience. It was thrilling to engage with an audience that was not just passive but eager to learn and grow alongside me. I created a community where elite athletes and brain injury survivors alike could find support, resources, and encouragement to reclaim their lives. What truly amazed me was the chance to interview transformational figures whom I had once only admired from afar.

I've had the honor and privilege of being able to interview many world-leading brain health experts, John Assaraf from Neuro Gym, Dr. Terry Nickelston from Stop Chasing Pain, and Dr. John Demartini. This helps me deepen my understanding of personal growth, healing, and the infinite potential we all possess. Each interview was not just a professional achievement; it was a testament to how far I had come.

A Small Setback For A Major Comeback

I learned that every setback you encounter creates the seeds for a future comeback. It is up to you to learn the hard lessons and to transmute the negative energy into gold like an alchemist. I learned that everything we do on a moment-to-moment basis during everyday matters adds up. That every setback you encounter creates the seeds for a future comeback. It is up to you to learn the hard lessons and to transmute the negative energy into gold like an alchemist. I got back to reality and the more I studied, the more I felt a calling to use my experiences to help others.

My life is incredible now. I am really living the dream, so they say. During and after jail, I studied diligently and incredibly hard almost every day! In 2024, I finally ended up completing my PhD in natural medicine and neurorehabilitation. I am now helping 1000s of concussion survivors from around the world become symptom-free and heal their brains naturally, without pills or risky surgeries.

Now, I stand here not just as a survivor but as someone who turned his pain into purpose. I'm proud to say that my mistakes are far from my story's final chapter. It's just one page in a book that's still being written, one that now includes the lives I've touched, the people I've helped, and the peace I've finally found within myself. Every scar, every misstep, and every painful memory serves as a reminder of where I came from and why I fight so hard to lift others out of their own darkness. I encourage you to rise up, Warrior! No matter how far you have fallen, you can always pick yourself back up. You can change your life's trajectory today, one small step at a time! Change your energy; you change your life!

To connect with Dr Brody Miller and receive excellent resources scan the QR code.

ABOUT THE AUTHOR

BRODY MILLER

SCAN TO KNOW MORE

Connect With Me, My Friend

Dr. Brody Miller, PhD (@drbrodymiller), is a globally recognized brain rehabilitation expert and number one international best-selling author. After conquering his own battle with a traumatic brain injury and brain surgery, Dr. Miller forged the revolutionary R.E.B.O.U.N.D. Method—a 90-day blueprint that redefines brain recovery by harnessing the principles of neuroplasticity and advanced cognitive rehabilitation. With a following of over 200,000, he's guided thousands of concussion survivors from struggle to strength, restoring clarity, resilience, and purpose.

CHAPTER 13

Against All Odds:

A Tibetan Refugee's Journey to Entrepreneurial Triumph and Global Impact

TENZIN CHODON

A Tibetan Who Never Saw Tibet

Whenever I tell people that my homeland is Tibet, I see their eyes light up with images of a serene, mystical land. They envision snow-clad Himalayan peaks, ancient monasteries perched on mountaintops, young monks in crimson robes scurrying through courtyards, and mystics lost in deep meditation. They imagine a place untouched by the world's troubles, where life is simple, content, and harmonious.

But the reality of Tibet today starkly contrasts with that idyllic vision. In 1959, after the illegal invasion of Tibet by the Chinese government, His Holiness the 14th Dalai Lama, along with approximately 50,000 Tibetans—including my grandparents—fled our homeland. They risked everything, dodging bullets and braving the treacherous journey from Tibet into India.

My family's history is marked by the brutality of that time. The Chinese soldiers targeted rulers and administrators first, and because our family hailed from the royal lineage of a small region in Tibet, we became targets. For the safety of my relatives who still reside there, I won't reveal the name of my clan or the region. My grandfather, a young prince at the time, managed to escape from Tibet to India.

Amidst the chaos and despair of this harrowing escape, a story of love emerged. My grandparents found each other during their flight to freedom and fell in love, a beacon of hope in an otherwise dark chapter of our history. India, newly independent and with its own struggles, extended a gracious hand, offering a safe haven to Tibetan refugees.

The Ordeals of a Refugee

Imagine the challenge of starting life anew in a foreign land, having lost everything—your country, your roots, your sense of belonging. You don't speak the language, you don't understand the culture, and everything about this new place feels alien. My mother was born in a Tibetan refugee settlement in India, as were her siblings. As the middle child, she often sought attention by being mischievous—a trait I suspect I've inherited.

Like my mother, I too was born and raised in a Tibetan refugee settlement in southern India. We shared a common struggle—**an identity crisis that gnawed at us**. My mother was a Tibetan who had never seen her homeland, yet India felt like home because it was all she had ever known. Still, there was always a sense of not fully belonging, a reminder that we were foreigners living in a land that, while kind, was not our own. We looked different, spoke a different language, and practiced a culture that set us apart from the local population.

I felt this deeply too. India is in my heart, and I am profoundly grateful for the refuge it provided my people. But I often felt caught between two worlds.

As I navigated these questions of identity, I also began to understand the weight of the **generational trauma** that my family and our community carried. My grandparents had experienced the trauma of losing their homeland, and that pain had been passed down to my parents and, in turn, to me. While I had never lived through the horrors of the Chinese invasion or the hardships of fleeing Tibet, I felt the emotional scars of that history.

The trauma of displacement was not just about the loss of a physical homeland—it was about the loss of a sense of security, of belonging, of knowing who you are and where you come from. For my grandparents and parents, the experience of being uprooted had been deeply traumatic, and that trauma had shaped their worldview. They had instilled in me a deep sense of caution, of always being aware of the fragility of our situation. We were refugees, and that meant we could never take anything for granted.

This sense of uncertainty was something I had internalized from a young age. I had grown up knowing that our situation was temporary, that we were living in exile, and that one day we might have to move again. This uncertainty created a kind of emotional distance, a feeling that I could never fully put down roots, because our future was always in question.

But as I grew older, I realized that this mindset was not sustainable. I couldn't live my life in a constant state of anxiety, always fearing that everything could be taken away at any moment. I had to find a way to reconcile my identity as a Tibetan in exile with the reality of my life in India. I had to find a way to build a sense of stability and belonging, even in the face of uncertainty.

The more I reflected on my identity, the more I realized that being Tibetan was not just about our culture or our history—it was about our resilience. My family's story, like the stories of so many Tibetans in exile, was one of survival against all odds. We had lost our homeland, but we had not lost our sense of self. We had found ways to preserve our culture and pass it on to the next generation, despite the challenges of living in exile.

But even as I took pride in our resilience, I couldn't ignore the fact that our situation was precarious. The Tibetan community in exile was aging, and many of the older generation had passed away without ever seeing their homeland again. The younger generation, including myself, had never been to Tibet, and we were increasingly influenced by the cultures of the countries we had grown up in. There was a fear that, over time, our unique identity as Tibetans in exile might be lost.

Overcoming Generational Trauma & Creating a Legacy

As Tibetan refugees, our people had been conditioned to focus on survival rather than thriving. The invasion and subsequent exile had not just displaced us physically but had also eroded our collective confidence. Many of our youth adopted a mindset of limitation, believing, **"We are refugees. We must stay within our boundaries. We can't do much; after all, we don't even have a country."**

But I knew I was meant for more. I felt a burning desire to awaken my people from this sleep, to empower them to dream bigger, to take steps toward progress and reclaim the spirit that had been suppressed for too long. The invasion may have taken our land, but it's up to us to reclaim our dreams and our future.

I knew early on that I was destined to break new ground in my community—to be a pioneer who would shatter the shackles of the victim mindset that often comes with being a refugee. I wanted to empower other Tibetan refugees to realize that we could do more than just survive; we could thrive.

Growing up, I was the quintessential trophy child—polished, praised, and paraded for my achievements. The relentless expectation to excel at everything became an overwhelming burden. Academics, singing, dancing, art, public speaking, writing, sports—no domain was off-limits. While others may have been forced to study, I didn't need to be pushed. My love for knowledge and my innate curiosity kept me moving forward, but the pressure to always succeed became suffocating. The pursuit of perfection had seeped into my very being, instilled by a family whose intentions, though well-meaning, led to a crushing weight on my young shoulders.

There came a time, though, when I could no longer bear the thought of being anything less than perfect. Mediocrity was unthinkable, and yet, deep inside, I knew something was terribly wrong. My identity had become entangled in a cycle of winning, achieving, and excelling—fueled by the silent expectations and constant pressure of those around me. I forgive them for it, knowing they are only human and humans make mistakes. But that pressure, relentless as it was, scarred my mental health.

What saved me from the brink? Books. In their pages, I found refuge. I lost myself in the lives of extraordinary individuals who had battled their own demons, fears, and limitations. Knowledge became my escape, a source of comfort that offered me more than just facts—it gave me a sense of purpose, a quiet thrill, a kind of intellectual euphoria. But soon, my quest for knowledge took on a new dimension. The more I read, the more I felt drawn toward something deeper—a spiritual thirst to understand the divine.

The pressure to achieve had left me searching for meaning beyond accolades, and so I turned to religious texts, scriptures from various faiths across the world, seeking answers that school could never offer. In the early 2000s, there were no lessons on emotional resilience, no guidance on how to navigate life's storms. But through my exploration of these ancient teachings, I came to realize a profound truth: we are all searching for a higher purpose.

Suddenly, the pressures and challenges I had faced seemed smaller, more insignificant in the grand scheme of things. My journey shifted inward, leading me to a deeper understanding of myself and my place in the world. I realized that my true purpose wasn't in excelling for the sake of it, but in serving others—lifting those who needed it most. In that realization, I found a new way of seeing life, one that was no longer driven by perfection, but by purpose. My path became one of compassion, of connection, and of embracing a higher calling that transcended personal achievement.

It was in my teenage years that **I truly discovered my purpose**. That's when I found my sense of direction, a calling to represent and uplift my people. Academically, I excelled, and I had a natural gift for languages, becoming a proficient polyglot by the age of 14. My passion for learning extended beyond books, especially in the realms of quantum physics and spirituality, and I was equally captivated by the art of communication.

When Facebook was in vogue, I saw it as an opportunity to expand my horizons. The platform allowed me to connect with people from all corners of the globe, and I embraced it wholeheartedly. My curiosity about different cultures and languages fueled my interactions online, where I honed my communication skills and became adept at cross-cultural dialogue. Living in Karnataka, a southern state of India where my family had settled as Tibetan refugees, I made it a point to learn the regional language, Kannada, in addition to my native Tibetan.

At just 15, I was appointed as a translator for various campaigns organized by the regional Tibetan administration, translating between Kannada and Tibetan. I became a bridge between the Tibetan refugee community and the local Indian population, serving as a spokesperson for my people. While my peers were enjoying their summer vacations, I found myself in board meetings with ministers, discussing policies and attending political conferences. I was translating between regional Indian ministers and Tibetan officials at an age when most were concerned with school exams and social outings. Looking back in hindsight, I'm grateful for the early exposure to the world of communications, though it also made me feel like an old soul in a young body.

Conversations with my teenage friends often felt out of place, and I gravitated towards friendships with people twice my age. Despite being bright, confident, and extroverted, I couldn't quite fit in with my peers. But there was something greater that always kept me moving forward—my higher purpose.

I'll never forget one afternoon when two Indian ministers and a Tibetan official visited my home. They brought a box of Peda, a traditional Indian sweet. When my mother told them I was still at school, they eagerly handed her the sweets and said, "We wanted to give you these because your daughter has done something incredible! Her translation and communication skills have so impressed the Superintendent of Police that he's expedited the legal documentation process for Tibetan refugees. **Her words didn't just convey a message—they changed his perspective on Tibetans."**

When I got home and heard the story from my mother, I felt a surge of pride and a newfound sense of confidence. I realized that my linguistic abilities and talents were more than just skills—they were tools I could use to be a voice for my community.

Driven by this realization, I decided to give back by teaching underprivileged Tibetan children. I offered free English lessons and provided training in communication and other essential soft skills. I taught at Tibetan schools, sharing what I had learned with the next generation, determined to equip them with the tools they needed to break free from the limitations of their circumstances.

As my exposure grew, so did the opportunities that came my way—opportunities I never could have imagined. It was the power of word-of-mouth and the strength of my work that opened doors I hadn't even known existed. People were so impressed with my work that they began to recommend me for prestigious opportunities. By the age of 16, I was already an emcee for corporate events, political gatherings, and high-profile conferences. At 18, I was traveling across the country to speak at institutions and corporate companies. I was invited to train entrepreneurs, top-tier industrialists, and professionals in communication and public speaking, working with the crème de la crème of society.

As a translator, I had the profound honor of meeting His Holiness the 14th Dalai Lama. One moment stands out above all others: it was 2018, and I was serving as both the translator and compere for a prestigious event. When the event concluded, His Holiness approached me, placed his hand gently on my head, and said, "Good job, my child. You make us all proud. We shall meet again soon." He then shook my hand, and in that instant, I felt a surge of energy so powerful that I didn't wash my hand that night—I wanted to hold onto that blessing, that positive force, for as long as possible. True to His word, we did meet again. In 2022, I had the immense privilege of interviewing His Holiness on my podcast.

These encounters weren't just milestones on my résumé; they were transformative experiences that shaped the very essence of who I am today. They forged Tenzin Chodon. His Holiness often teaches that we must serve all sentient beings with compassion because suffering is a universal experience, and so is the power of love. His wisdom ignited within me a deep desire to contribute something meaningful to our people and to the world.

Before moving to Canada and establishing **Le Prestige Academy**—now recognized as one of North America's premier finishing schools—I was in Mumbai, dedicated to my work as a soft skills coach. Those early years were foundational, not just for perfecting my craft but for solidifying my life's mission: to empower others to realize their highest potential.

I began to understand that my achievements as a Tibetan in this field could transcend personal success. They could serve as a beacon of hope and possibility for others in my community. **If I could break through barriers and thrive in spaces that once seemed inaccessible, then I could inspire other Tibetans to do the same.** I could empower them to walk confidently into rooms that once felt out of reach, to network with the affluent, and to collaborate with the best in the world. But beyond that, I could help us represent.

When we succeed as a community, we do more than uplift ourselves—we amplify the voice of our people. We share our stories, our struggles, and our resilience on the world stage, telling our narrative in our own words. Success is not just about individual accomplishment; it's about creating a ripple effect that touches everyone around us, transforming our collective future.

We have faced generational trauma, but we are so much more than our trauma.

When I delivered my first **TEDx talk** in Mumbai, I was the only Tibetan on stage. The same was true for my second TEDx talk. But I don't want to be the only one. I want to see more Tibetans taking the lead, stepping into these spaces with confidence.

During the pandemic, I was in Mumbai, and I made it my mission to connect with my people and offer them something that could change their lives. I launched a Free English Programme online and taught over 500 Tibetans. For many in the older generation, English has always been a barrier. But now, with this training, they could read signs at airports, ask for directions, and engage in conversations that are vital in today's world. Young Tibetans gained the confidence to excel in job interviews, build cross-cultural friendships, and seize opportunities on a global scale.

When I launched my podcast, **"The Tenzin Show,"** I chose the name with a clear intention. I wanted the world to know that a Tibetan was behind this project, representing not just myself but an entire community. As the podcast grew, so did my mission. I realized that my efforts couldn't be confined to empowering only my community—I wanted to reach anyone who needed guidance, hope, or inspiration.

"The Tenzin Show" was born from that expanded vision. During the pandemic, I created this platform to inspire people across the globe, delving into the lives of passionate achievers and sharing their success stories from all walks of life. The show resonates with ordinary individuals who dare to dream and strive for success. Its core mission is to uplift and empower people with a message of positivity, showing them that success is within reach for anyone who dares to pursue it.

I've had the privilege of interviewing eminent personalities from diverse industries, including Hollywood and Bollywood celebrities, industrialists, scientists, high-performance athletes, entrepreneurs, world-renowned chefs, social workers, authors, speakers, and more. Through these conversations, my mission expanded beyond just helping my community to touch lives globally. The podcast's success was such that top publications and news media outlets took notice, reviewing it with praise. Today, "The Tenzin Show" has listeners around the world.

Yet, in the midst of all this, I ignored something critical—my health. **I was diagnosed with Hypothyroidism and**

PCOS, which felt like a nightmare. I suffered from anxiety attacks, breathing issues, depression, acne, weight gain, and more. There were days when I avoided leaving the house because I couldn't face the world. For someone who was an overachieving, extroverted, and confident woman, this was the darkest period of my life. I was drained of energy and questioned how I could serve others when I wasn't well myself. I realized I had pushed myself too hard, driven by over-ambition, without taking time to appreciate life's simple moments, to relax, and to recharge. The first three years of living with these conditions were incredibly difficult. The greatest challenge was breaking free from this cycle.

But then, the words of His Holiness echoed in my ears, and I made a decision: I would change my life for good.

Spirituality became the cornerstone of my healing. My higher purpose motivated me to unleash my best self. I shifted my perspective—I was not a victim; this was a phase molding my character. As I changed my mindset, my body began to heal. Though my healing journey is ongoing, I've come to understand that life itself is a journey of constant healing and growth.

With renewed energy and health, I embarked on a new chapter of my life in Canada. Starting from zero once again, I worked as a public speaking coach for an e-learning platform. But soon, I felt the call to create something of my own. I decided to start my own company—Le Prestige Academy—and I registered it on my birthday to mark the beginning of something truly memorable.

It was time to apply everything I had learned from working with the best of the best to my new life in Canada. Some Tibetans I met suggested I play it safe, that I should consider working in stores or cafes like many refugees do. While I have deep respect for those who take on such roles, I was clear about my purpose. I came to Canada with a vision: to build a successful company, to create a legacy for my people, to make a name for myself and for Tibetans, and to open new avenues for them. And that's exactly what I set out to do.

My efforts paid off. **I was ranked among North America's top business speakers and coaches,** listed alongside luminaries like Tony Robbins and Robert Kiyosaki. I was nominated for the Women Empowerment Awards Canada in the leadership category and for the prestigious Royal Bank of Canada's Women of Influence Awards.

I had no contacts, no clear path to success, but I persevered. Despite coming from a background where we were conditioned to see ourselves as victims—Tibetan refugees facing countless odds—and despite severe health challenges, I stand here today, having built something remarkable.

I became a distinguished public speaking and soft skills coach, transforming the careers of entrepreneurs, professionals, and leaders. With over a decade of experience, I've empowered countless professionals to secure job promotions, deliver impactful presentations, and enhance workplace communication. I help entrepreneurs master investor pitches, deliver compelling keynotes, land TEDx talks, and navigate media interviews.

Under my guidance, professionals don't just refine their communication skills—they master the art of professional etiquette, body language, and polished presentation. My unique approach, which infuses ancient Tibetan wisdom with the science of communication and personal image, has made me a beacon of excellence in the realm of soft skills coaching. I even incorporate Tibetan meditation techniques to boost self-confidence and improve communication skills, offering a one-of-a-kind, transformative experience.

I feel an immense sense of fulfillment when my clients from diverse backgrounds and cultures share their stories of success. It reassures me that I am doing my best to live by the teachings of His Holiness the 14th Dalai Lama. I believe he would be proud to know that I have co-authored this book with Marco and other incredible personalities.

But my journey doesn't end here. I am still on a path of self-discovery, still searching for ways to help others. Today, I continue to navigate the complexities of my identity as a Tibetan in exile. I am proud of my heritage, but I am also open to the ways in which my identity is shaped by my experiences in the present. I continue to engage with my community, to honor the legacy of my ancestors, and to advocate for the rights of Tibetans and other displaced people around the world.

At the same time, I have learned to embrace the uncertainty of life. I may never return to Tibet, but I have found a sense of home within myself. I know that my identity is not defined by geography or political borders—it is defined by my experiences, my values, and the relationships I have built along the way.

As I look to the future, I am filled with a sense of hope. I know that the journey of exile is not an easy one, but I also know that it has given me strength, resilience, and a deeper understanding of what it means to be human. My story is just one of many, and together, we are all searching for a place to call home.

This is Tenzin Chodon, and this is my story of resilience, hope, and courage.

The challenges I had to face were profound, deeply personal, and intertwined with my identity as a Tibetan refugee. These weren't just obstacles—they were battles against long-standing limitations, both internal and external.

Generational Trauma and Identity Crisis of Being a Tibetan Refugee:

As a Tibetan refugee, I carried the weight of generational trauma. Being part of a displaced community with no homeland brought a profound sense of loss and confusion about my identity. I often grappled with the question: *Who am I, and where do I belong?* The narratives around me spoke of struggle, survival, and suffering, but rarely of success and empowerment. Growing up in the shadow of this trauma, I felt caught between two worlds—one defined by the rich culture and traditions of Tibet, and the other shaped by the uncertainties of refugee life.

Mental Limitations Set by My Own Community:

Another significant challenge was the mental barriers imposed by my own community. There was a deeply ingrained belief that as refugees, we couldn't achieve much.

Without a country to call our own, we were often seen as temporary residents, outsiders who would never fully belong or succeed. The unspoken message was clear: keep your ambitions modest, because the world doesn't expect much from you.

Health Challenges That Eroded My Confidence:

My health posed one of the most overwhelming challenges, affecting not just my physical well-being but my emotional and mental health too. I was diagnosed with Hypothyroidism and Polycystic Ovary Syndrome (PCOS), conditions that brought with them a cascade of other issues. I struggled with extreme fatigue, hormonal imbalances, weight fluctuations, and the constant drain of energy. Simple everyday tasks, which I once took for granted, became monumental hurdles. My skin erupted with severe acne, undermining my confidence. On top of that, breathing difficulties began to plague me, making physical activities difficult and adding to my frustration. The anxiety triggered by these health issues often made everything feel even worse. At times, I felt as though my body was working against me, and the weight of it all began to suffocate my spirit.

No Precedent in My Community for What I Set Out to Do:

One of the hardest challenges was the lack of a blueprint. No one in my Tibetan refugee community had ever done what I set out to do—become a professional public speaker, entrepreneur, and founder of a finishing school. There were no role models to follow, no paths laid out before me. The absence of representation often made me feel isolated and uncertain.

Breaking Stereotypes About Tibetans:

Lastly, I confronted the stereotypes that often surrounded Tibetans—those that painted us as passive, reserved, or merely survivors of our circumstances. These stereotypes didn't reflect the strength, resilience, or ambitions of the Tibetan people I knew. But changing these narratives wasn't easy.

How I Overcame It:

I took it upon myself to become an active voice in shifting these perceptions. As a public speaker, I shared my story not just as an individual journey, but as a testament to the strength and potential of the Tibetan community. I focused on storytelling as a means of advocacy, highlighting the accomplishments and spirit of Tibetans around the world. I became involved in initiatives that showcased Tibetan culture in new, dynamic ways. Through these efforts, I contributed to changing the way the world saw us—not as victims, but as a people with immense talent, determination, and vision for the future.

To connect with Tenzin scan the QR code

ABOUT THE AUTHOR

TENZIN CHODON

SCAN TO KNOW MORE

Tenzin Chodon stands as a paragon of sophistication and influence, leading some of the world's most ambitious individuals and elite organizations to unprecedented heights of success. As the visionary founder and CEO of Le Prestige Academy, Canada's premier luxury finishing school, she has revolutionized the landscape of personal and professional excellence. With a distinguished, globe-spanning career as a keynote speaker, public speaking coach, and media trainer, Tenzin has become a sought-after authority in elite communications. Her insights, captured in two TEDx talks and her role as a United Nations SDG Ambassador, highlight her conviction that true success is rooted in emotional intelligence, cultural awareness, and the power of transformative communication. Ranked among Microsoft's Top Ten Business Speakers in North America, alongside icons like Robert Kiyosaki and Tony Robbins, and nominated for RBC's Women of Influence and Women Empowerment Awards in the Leadership category, Tenzin's impact is undeniable. Her bespoke training programs are tailored for individuals who seek to excel in both personal and professional realms, empowering countless professionals to secure job promotions, deliver impactful presentations, and enhance workplace communications. Through her coaching, entrepreneurs master investor pitches, deliver impactful keynotes, and handle media interviews with confidence and poise.

CHAPTER 14

Why

I Divorced My Family.

NICHOLAS GRAHAM

DISCLAIMER

This chapter is a reflection of my personal experiences, thoughts, and emotions. While it draws upon real events, it is presented from my perspective and should not be taken as a definitive account of the events or individuals involved.

To respect the privacy of others, no names or identifying details have been included. Any resemblance to actual persons, living or deceased, is purely coincidental. This work is intended to share my journey and insights, not to assign blame or pass judgment.

If you pour yourself into the wrong things and put the needs of others before your own, you end up empty. This is the story of how I took back my power so I could pour all of it into making my dreams come true.

I was born in August of 1977 at Dudley Road Hospital in Birmingham. I had yellow jaundice so was in an incubator for three months. My mom stayed with me as much as she could but my dad was in and out of jail so frequently that I rarely saw him during my early years. I always wished he could have been around more.

My devotion to my family knew no end. I'd do anything for them - even when I was too young to take on the responsibility I still tried to because I wanted everyone to be happy.

The teachers at the nursery didn't speak to me well. There was no comfort in their voices, no softness in their eyes. I didn't know what it was but I knew I didn't like it. I felt so much rage in my little body because of it and I didn't know how to express it but on my last day, I smashed every window of the nursery with stones I'd gathered. I didn't care about the consequences. All I could feel was the anger. I was five years old. My dad gave me a beating so severe I can still feel the sting of it today. But what hurt much more was his continual absence—the way he would be a ghost whenever the law caught up with him, distant when I needed him but then present when it suited.

By the time I was six, my brother Liam and I would walk ourselves to school because mom worked long hours at Saltley Market. She was rarely home until long after we got back. Liam was only 18 months older than me and we'd walk home from school each day, hoping mom would be there. She never was though so we were left to fend for ourselves.

We started stealing. My dad stole and all our friends did so I guess we saw it as normal. I always got blamed for stealing anyway, even if I hadn't! My Headteacher knew that some kids had broken into a school and stolen the instruments so he'd call me in, isolate me from the others and interrogate me.

Early in my childhood something important happened. It will probably seem insignificant to you, but to me it was everything. It was a school play and I was cast as the Little Teapot.

I was really bad at reading as a child so learning lines and getting on stage wasn't something I'd thought of myself doing but that one moment, dressed as a little teapot anchored something. I still remember how my mom's face lit up as I bellowed out the words, *"I'm a little teapot, short and stout.*

Here's my handle, here's my spout." For me they were the most powerful words in the world because for a few minutes, I felt like people could see my heart.

Those lyrics would become like a mantra for me. Life would "tip me over and pour me out" more times than I could imagine, but everytime it did, it would give me more to pour back into myself and my dreams.

Tip Me Over and Pour Me Out

Soon after the play, mom moved us to Ward End, hoping to escape my dad who was always knocking her about and also, Handsworth. She was worried about the crime kids were getting involved in there and wanted me and my brother as far away from it as possible. But the house we moved into was bleak—mouldy walls, no wallpaper and a bathtub filled with clothes instead of water. I didn't have a bath for years. It wasn't much of a fresh start. My mom's depression only worsened, and there were days when she couldn't get out of bed at all. I wanted so badly to make my mom happy. I wanted to protect her - but I was just a little kid and I didn't know how.

One Parent's evening, my teacher said I would never be able to read or write properly and it broke something inside me. I felt like I was destined to fail so when mom spotted an ad in the newspaper for Oliver Twist and wanted me to audition, I couldn't bring myself to do it.

Some of the happiest memories were Christmases at my nans because all the family would be there and I loved being around them - especially my favourite aunty Bernice who was a big presence in my life. I saw her as a 'black Mary

Poppins' because, somehow, no matter how hard life was she always made things seem just a bit better.

On my 11th birthday she got married and decided to move to London. I was told she was sick of caring for my nan who, in her fifties, seemed to have already given up on life. Aunty Bernice would have to care for her as if she was in her nineties and apparently, she wanted to escape. When she left the family went to ruin. There were no more Christmases at nans' and things were never the same.

I went to army cadets when I was 12. I was too young to be there but I somehow talked my way in. Sergeant Major Smith was a big body builder who turned out to be the training partner of a six time Mr Olympia. I remember saying to myself *"I want to look like that."* and at 13 years of age I bought my first set of weights and started lifting. I'd channel my anger and frustration into those weights and it felt good because it was something I could control. I really wanted to do boxing but there was never anyone to do it with. Lifting weights was something I didn't need anyone else for.

At 13, I was already physically stronger than most men but I didn't know how to handle my strength. I also carried an emotional weight around every day - a dangerous combination. I started selling drugs because my cousin Robert got me into it. He trusted me because I didn't smoke or get involved in the things most of the people around me did. From the ages of 13 to 15 I was supplying my entire area. Ward End wasn't big, but I knew everyone and it gave me a power and recognition many wanted. But I didn't want to be a part of that world, it's just something I did to help out.

All my friends were drug dealers, car thieves and laptop thieves. It was a lifestyle for them but I just wanted to be able to buy my own clothes and school uniforms. I always liked to be able to look after myself so my mom wouldn't have to worry about it. I told myself that I'd stop selling drugs when I left school and could get a job. I got a job as an apprentice upholsterer making 3 piece suites and true to my word, I left selling drugs behind me and never looked back.

Working as an upholsterer was hard physical work—but there was something about it that grounded me. It was simple, repetitive and there was no room for lies or shortcuts.

I wasn't getting rich, but I didn't need to. Best of all, I managed to get Liam a job there too. Although the pay wasn't great— it was a start and I could feel my self-worth slowly growing. Every hour I spent working in that workshop felt like an hour spent building something bigger than just a chair or a sofa. It felt like I was building the foundation of a new life.

My dad had done one of his robberies and given my brother a load of money again. One of my friends had come around to tell me about this pyramid scheme which sounded amazing and for about a month or two I felt like this was it! Even my mom could see the shift in me. As silly as it might sound, this was a real turning point in my life because, as I would soon learn, not even drugs could make me feel as high as having the opportunity to follow a dream!

On my 16th birthday I went to a Jungle rave with all my friends and ended up taking my first ecstasy pill. I paid £10 and went off and took it by myself. No one else was into drugs. Just me. That night set me on a path of taking drugs and hanging around the rave scene. I remember walking around the clubs with so much aggression, fearlessly banging into some of the baddest men in Handsworth. I saw that, at 16 they could already see something in me that they didn't want to test. When I look back now I realise how lucky I am to still be here. I got myself into some scrapes but the drugs never took hold of me. I enjoyed them, but I could just stop taking them whenever I wanted to.

One day Liam just left. He didn't say anything. He just went. He'd been with his girlfriend Jen since he was 13 and she had a flat so he left to be with her and never looked back. It hurt but I understood and I was glad he was happy.

Just before I turned 18 I got a job at my aunty Margaret's shop - "The Cave". It was in Browning Street in Ladywood and was one of the first convenience stores in the area to stay open until 3 or 4am. Aunty Margaret was a real go-getter. She started off working in Saltley Market selling makeup and then somehow ended up running a florist which was one of the first in Birmingham to go to Interflora. I really respected her even when she went from selling flowers to setting up a sex chat line in the back of her shop!

My mom never did those calls but she did manage the place. I ended up sleeping with quite a lot of the girls that worked there and my aunty didn't like that. But I didn't like the way she used to speak to my mom. She'd treat her like she was nothing and I hated it.

In 1995 my dads sister, Aunty Felicity, was diagnosed with cancer. I'd always been close to her. She had a real energy about her. She taught me to be quick-witted, to think ahead and stand up for myself. There was a cyst growing inside her stomach. The doctors cut it out but a month or so after she died very suddenly. I was devastated.

Two years later my cousin Stephen passed away. He'd taken a blow to his head while he was in jail and ended up with multiple sclerosis. He also deteriorated so fast - first having a walking stick, then a wheelchair. It was horrible. Sometime around then I met a woman called Tanya at my cousin Robert's house. She was 6 years older than me and I liked her. One thing led to another and she told me she was pregnant. I didn't respond well and asked for a DNA test. I didn't see her again for quite a while.

Two years passed by and my Uncle Arnold also passed. It felt like our family was cursed! It was especially hard on my cousin Kim so I ended up moving in with her for a while to try and help her. Tanya's sister May was at the funeral and I noticed she had a baby. I was happy for her because I knew she couldn't have children. Little did I know there was more to that story that I wouldn't find out until years later.

One day a man came into the shop and told me he had a scheme with the government doing carpentry. I ended up getting on a college course with him and getting a carpentry apprenticeship. After a month I managed to get my brother a job too. In the end it turned out the guy running it was scamming the council out of funds but I got the qualifications I wanted.

I remember having a chat with a friend on the course about what he was going to do when he qualified and he said he was going to build huts in the army. Because I'd been in the Cadets before I took myself down to the Army Careers place to find out more.

In one of those strange twists of fate it was also a Sergeant Smith at the careers centre. The irony wasn't lost on me after Sergeant Major Smith at the Cadets! I told him I wanted to be an Engineer in the Army and he told me I would have to take the Barb test. I didn't qualify but he told me there was a pioneer platoon with the infantry at the Staffordshire regiment.

I weighed about sixteen and a half stone and after checking my weight he said I'd have to lose three stone because I was too heavy for my height. He gave me all the paperwork and sent me on my way. I turned around to see him throw my papers in the bin like he felt like he'd wasted his time. I decided I was going to prove him wrong.

It wasn't easy to lose the weight but I worked really hard and after three months I'd done it and went back to see Sergeant Smith. He told me I had to lose another stone. Apparently he hadn't told me the full amount because he'd assumed I wouldn't do it if I knew. I wanted to tell him I saw him throw my paperwork in the bin - but nonetheless, I lost the remaining weight.

During selection at ATR Lichfield I was told that my record for heaves to chest sat alongside Chris Akabusi and Dame Kelly Holmes who got the record for running the mile and a half. I remember the way the PTs looked at me that day - like I was God or something and honestly, I felt like it too. The kid that had only ever been told he'd "never amount to anything" just did something that stood up next to some of the world's highest achieving athletes? The fact that it was soldiers looking at me this way meant even more because soldiers don't give you their respect easily.

After that the Major pulled me to one side and asked me if I wanted the job and that I was special. This was the first time I'd heard these words in my life and coming from such a great man they meant a lot. The army was challenging but at the same time it was one of the most rewarding times of my life. I even got into intercompany boxing. Boxing had been something I wanted to do since I was 13 and I found myself walking into a theatre to the sound of army drums to fight in front of around 700 people. I went on to become the Staffordshire Regiment super heavyweight boxing champion.

I met the Queen in 2002. I was standing right next to the Major who test piloted and commissioned the Apache aircraft in England. If you were watching the Golden Jubilee you'll have seen me. There was something so surreal about that moment and I was buzzing. After that I did the Lance Corporal course. It was tough. I had to deal with some serious egos and took so much abuse from people it's a miracle I didn't snap. Worse still, I failed every appointment I was assigned but I refused to give up. When Sergeant Des O'Connor told me I'd passed I nearly fell over in shock. He said that even though I failed every appointment "they couldn't teach what I did." Again, having these words of affirmation said by such a high-standing man was humbling. This is when I really started to understand the power of resilience.

Soon after that I got posted to Kosovo. The army had always said they could see I was holding back so on riot training day I let them see what I had inside me. I held nothing back and let the lid off but as a result, I got kicked off riot training for being too violent. That rage that had been inside me since nursery was too much for even the army to handle. Some people had a negative perception of me after that and others wanted to challenge me because of it, so my time in the army wasn't easy. Nonetheless, I made some good friends and had experiences that shaped me as a man. However, my journey with cocaine also began there.

When I finally returned to England so much was falling into place for me. I bought two cars and a cottage in Wales and it was all going really well but my world fell apart when I bumped into Tanya again and she told me that she'd given Miles to her sister when he was a baby. He was now 5 years old. I realised that the baby I'd seen her sister with at my Uncle Arnold's funeral was him. I felt so hurt and confused. Tanya said she did it because she didn't like the way I'd spoken to her and because I wouldn't have been able to look after him but this wasn't true. The army would have supported me to take care of my son! Around the same time my dad ended up getting locked up again so I was in a very low place just at the same time when my regiment was looking to go to Iraq with me full-time in a commander's role. The timing couldn't have been worse.

I handed in my 12 months notice but to cope with how I felt I started taking more drugs. I felt like a disgrace. This was one of the all-time lows in my life but I did manage to leave the army intact. I was 27 by now and got a job on an oil rig in Aberdeen. I started the training but only lasted a day because my tolerance levels on my drug and alcohol test came back too high. I flew home in disgrace and told my family I'd failed due to weight. I started drinking. In fact, I barely stopped. I felt like a failure. One of the doormen who had been one of my first training partners was worried and called my brother. My brother called and cried on the phone. I told him I felt lost but that conversation didn't change anything. Little did I know, it was all about to come to a head.

One day I took 10 or 12 pills, as well as loads of cocaine and alcohol. I was walking along and I heard a voice say "Nick. Stop! You've had too much. You need to go home. You're gonna kill yourself."

I remember wondering where the voice had come from, but I listened and went home. Another time I woke up thinking that I was in bed before realising that actually my TT was rammed into a metal park bench on the side of the road. I reversed the car back and went to a nightclub. That's how messed up I was. After clubbing I called the insurance company and told them I'd been in a crash. I said I'd left the car in gear and it had jumped forward into the bench when I turned it on. That's what I told my family too.

It continued like this for some time but one night, after a few drinks I was driving back to my mom's and the police pulled me over to breathalyse me. I lost my driver's licence and sold the car. I knew I'd end up in jail if I drove while I was banned.

To get some money coming in I did some work for my Auntie Margaret. By now she had a business helping immigrants get into education and rehoused and I did her property management. Around this time I was on Facebook a lot and met the woman I ended up with for the next seven or eight years. I'll call her "Mrs Perry" because she's a very quiet and private woman. She had Louis who was two and a half and Kai who was one at the time. I loved those kids with all my heart and they are the ones who taught me what it means to be a father.

Around this time the final nail in the coffin happened when it came to my relationship with my own father. My cousin Robert had been diagnosed as schizophrenic years earlier after his mother (my aunt), father (my uncle) and brother (my cousin) passed away and something had happened which made his girlfriend Sarah ask me to change the lock.

Robert found out and accused me of sleeping with her, in fact, he also accused his older brother John and my dad too. One day I went to Kim's house and Sarah was there. My dad turned up a while after and we were all just talking when Robert arrived. He grabbed a 10-inch knife from the kitchen and started pointing it at my dad. Everybody started screaming but my dad just ran off and left all of us there. Robert came over to me, put the knife on my face and rubbed it down my throat and all around my neck. I don't know how I did it but I somehow managed to get out of the house safely. My relationship with my dad was never the same after that and I never felt comfortable in Robert's presence again.

Robert sadly ended up passing away in 2017 because he hadn't taken his medication properly so that was even more tragedy for my family to deal with. Plus I'd now mentally walked away from my relationship with both my brother and my father so I was feeling more isolated and alone than I ever had.

One New Year's Eve, just before the clock struck midnight my dad sent a message to the family Whatsapp group saying I wasn't his son. I felt devastated and couldn't believe what he had done. I'd never done anything other than love him and do whatever I could for him. That was the end for me.

Little Louis wasn't very good at maths at first but I was determined to help him. It didn't take long before he was a maths mastermind doing competitions! I was a proper "at home" dad to those boys. I wanted them to have the kind of father I never had so I was always there if they needed me. They knew they could ask me anything and I'd be there to support them.

Kai found reading and writing hard and one day he told me "The teacher goes too fast and she's always rushing me so I can't do it." I didn't want him to experience the same things I had so I went to parents evening and told the teacher he was feeling rushed. There was no way I was going to let him grow up feeling the way I did, believing he would never amount to anything.

Those kids saw my heart. My girlfriend sometimes thought I was just throwing money at stuff and trying to buy them, but they knew I was trying to provide what they needed. Buying stuff was my love language.

While I was living in Dudley with Mrs Perry and the kids I was doing a 32-mile round trip regularly just to check on my mom and nan because, even though Liam was more local to them, he would never go over, not even to sort the boiler. He and Jen would make excuses and say it was because of my mom's boyfriend Ted. Jen would go to Birmingham to take the kids to visit her mom but just send my mom a Mother's Day card. One day I saw a photo that made it clear Ted was up to no good. I challenged him and ended up kicking him out. Even with Ted gone still Liam never brought his kids to see my mom. I used to see how this destroyed her emotionally. She'd cry about it all the time.

A moment that everything changed for me was when my mom told me she was going to sell the house and give all the money to my brother because I've got no kids and he has. It finally hit me that it was time to put myself and my own happiness first. Everyone I'd spent a lifetime putting first had betrayed me and let me down. There were days I wanted to end it all. When you live by yourself you have to deal with yourself and if you don't feel like getting out of bed and you don't want to do anything with your day, there's no one there to help you snap out of it.

Pouring Into Myself and My Dreams

In the end, I decided to walk away from my family because it was the kindest thing for me to do for myself and also for them. I know that going on my own healing journey is the best way forward and I can't do that with all the drama going on in the background. Now the only person who can bother me is me. Nobody has been more unfair and horrible to me than I have. I've written myself off, abused myself with drugs and alcohol and allowed myself to make me feel so low I wanted to end my life. Also I've put the needs of other people - people who have never put me first - before my own.

I now know I'm here to do God's work which is why I'm telling my story. God has removed people from my life who I love with all my heart so I can focus on doing what I need to do. I love my family but they don't understand that there's no coming back from the things they did and the only way to move forward is to leave them alone and get on with my own life. You can't change your family but you can change the family and friends that are around you.

During covid I came across a live stream with Idris Elba critiquing somebody doing a scene from Casino and I just remember being captivated. I'd listen and think "I could do that." Even though I'd always struggled with reading there was a feeling that came from deep inside me that knew there was something in this for me.

One Christmas my friend Clay invited me over and it meant the world. I ended up telling him I would love to pursue a career as an actor. Speaking to him and Evie was what gave me the confirmation I needed. They spoke life into my dreams and sent me the phone number of a friend who was doing an improvisation class at the Rainbow in town. From there God made everything line up!

I was working two jobs at the time and I had been put on one right next to the Rainbow. I remember looking at the door and it was as if it was calling me to walk through it. So on the following Monday, that's what I did!

Suzette, the lady running the class, was the only other person there at first but I was grateful because I didn't find it easy at all! I did some improv and scene work and I couldn't even be a soldier! I forgot the lines constantly and felt really uncomfortable. There were times I didn't want to go but I told myself "No matter how stressed you feel about this Nick you can deal with it when you're actually in the building!" And of course, once I got in the room I'd just do what I needed to do!

I didn't let the uncomfortable feelings stop me from pursuing acting. I'd been fighting my whole life but for the first time, I was fighting for my dreams! Suzette noticed how my eyes would fill up with tears whenever I tried to read - all that childhood trauma would come up in these moments and I had no control over it.

In the end, she had me just follow along with everybody else but I loved it and just after Valentine's Day I decided to do the most loving thing I could for myself. I went in to work and gave in my notice because, although it had allowed me to retrain, it wasn't good for my mental health. Two weeks later I got a new job as a Tower Crane operator.

Then I saw Ashley Walters from So Solid Crew talking about Kingdom. He'd gone into partnership with a drama school to give back to underprivileged people who thought they could never be an actor.

I spoke to Suzette who said "Nick you've got nothing to lose! Go and find out if you can do it or not." So that's what I did. The audition was the 10th of April, my stepson Louis' birthday which I saw as a good omen.

We did some warm up exercises and I was given a scene called "Liam's apartment" playing a character called Liam who had just broken up with his girlfriend. Was this God speaking to me? How incredible was it that I was playing a character that had the same name as my brother on my stepson's birthday?

Two weeks later I found out I got in! I couldn't believe it! I was in drama school! I remember getting inside and walking around the studio doing breathing exercises and allowing it to sink in that I was really here living my dream!

The first thing I was assigned was a poem. Mine was "Among the Trees" by Marie Oliver and it was the first time I've ever been able to recite anything. For a whole minute and a half when I was reciting this poem my body and my head were just quiet. I finished my first term and continued into the second with Charlotte Brimble who helped me come into my own as an actor. Also, my friend Brendan who was also from Birmingham told me about his agent and how they'd got him on Spotlight. He was much more experienced than me so he had showreels and all sorts but he suggested I try calling them to see what they said as they were always looking for new people. That's how I ended up speaking to Robert Wilkinson, the CEO of Red Talent Management.

He gave me an interview with one of their agents and said I needed to prepare a monologue, tell a joke and sing a song! I won't pretend I wasn't nervous but I already had what I needed saved on my Instagram. I had saved a scene by Christopher Walken in PoolHall Junkies called The Lion's speech. I had already learned the script by watching it repeatedly, so that was my scene down. My joke was "Why is it when women wake up they always scratch their eyes?" And the punchline is "Because they don't have any balls to scratch."

And I even had a song from an audiobook by Danny Trejo called "Zippity do dah" that I decided to sing for my audition. The day came and I joined my friend Brendan as one of the first people at Kingdom to have our own agents and be on Spotlight!

That was huge for me because everybody was used to me seeing me struggle. I remember doing a scene with Sophie who really helped me with my lines. She said I couldn't have ended my term better if I tried and she was right. Even Charlotte Brimble was left open-mouthed because here was the guy who could never remember his lines "off book" and hitting all his beat changes!

For Term Three you had to choose your own monologue and I couldn't find one but Suzette, my dear friend from my improvisation class came up trumps for me when she found a piece called "The Narrative" by Anthony Bliss. But when I stood up in front of the class I started shaking. I had my phone in one hand and was shaking so much that I couldn't even read it. Luckily there was a break in the term so I had another four weeks to get it down.

Around this time my agent Connor got me one of my first in person auditions. It was at the Sky Comedy Rep. Although I didn't get the gig that time, they emailed to say they'd have me back to audition again so I was happy with that. Red Talent Management continues to put me in front of all of the right people for all the best auditions and I am so grateful and excited to find out what the future holds with them in my corner.

Lessons from my story

We have one chance at life and we have to invest in our dreams! When people betray you, hurt you or leave your life it doesn't cling on. Let them go because it means you have more energy to put into your dreams. Choose to pour into yourself instead of pouring more and more into trying to please others.

You're not on your own. We all go through struggles but it's what we do with the learning that matters. Don't give up on your dream. I'd love to connect with you on Instagram so come and find me and tell me YOUR dream too. Let's pursue them together.

Even if you're afraid, let go and let God. The fear is always there. Just make that decision and start moving towards what you want one step at a time. You might have moments when you feel like you're going backwards but if you just stay committed you will get there. You can feel the fear and you can still do it anyway and I really hope you do because, on the other side of your fear is that person you really want to be.

When you have bad days remember, whatever you're going through, it too shall pass.

I would never have believed you if you'd told me I'd be chasing my childhood dreams now at the age of 47 and that I'd be living my life like I'm 22 again but that's exactly what I'm doing. It's only possible though because I've taken back the love and power I used to invest in others so I can invest it into myself and what I want.

My whole life there's only been one thing I've ever wanted to be and that's better... and after everything I've been through, the only question for me to answer now is - how good can it get?

Connect with me on Instagram and tell me what YOUR dream is!

ABOUT THE AUTHOR

NICHOLAS GRAHAM

SCAN TO KNOW MORE

Nicholas Graham is on a mission to help you find out what happens when you pour your whole heart into the pursuit of your dreams. Nicholas speaks about resilience and the power of never giving up and is currently pursuing his dream of being an actor.

EPILOGUE

Your Journey to Start Over Continues

As you close this book, take a moment to honour the courage it took to delve into these stories of resilience and transformation and to come on this journey. You've seen how loss can turn into strength and how darkness can be the foundation for light. Perhaps you've felt the stirrings of your own comeback story as you turned these pages? Let this be the beginning of your next chapter—a chapter filled with purpose, power, and the realisation that **your story is far from over.**

Continue the Journey with the Next Edition

The journey doesn't end here. The next edition in the **"START OVER"** limited series will feature **14 more remarkable stories** of individuals who have turned unimaginable loss into spectacular comebacks. These new chapters will bring you even more insight, inspiration, and actionable tools to fuel your own transformation.

👉 **Pre-order the next edition in the series today** to secure your copy and continue building your comeback. Each book in this series is a rare and powerful resource, and copies are limited, so don't miss out!

Transform Your Life at a LIVE EVENT

Here's the ultimate gift for you:

As a token of gratitude, if you join the waitlist for the next book in the series and purchase that book too **you will receive a FREE ticket** to attend one of my **LIVE EVENTS** happening in cities around the world.

💎 **Value Stacked Live Event – $1,000 value** 💎

Your past does NOT define you. Your COMEBACK does.

This is the event that will change everything.

Join Sir Marco Robinson and 10 guest speakers for a high-energy, no-BS, transformational event where you'll learn to turn your biggest challenges into your greatest success story—and build a high-impact, high-income personal brand.

This one-day transformational event is designed to inspire, empower, and equip you with tools to create the comeback story of your dreams.

You'll:

- **Meet me, Sir Marco Robinson, and some of the extraordinary authors** featured in this book series.
- **Hear exclusive live stories** of transformation, told directly from the authors themselves, that will ignite your belief in what's possible.

- **Gain revolutionary tools and strategies** to crush your goals, overcome setbacks, and rewrite your story with strength and purpose.
- **Network with like-minded warriors** who are also on their own comeback journeys—build connections that will fuel your growth.
- **Be part of a community that believes in you, your dreams, and your power to rise again.**

PLUS: Bonus Gifts Worth $997 just for attending!

1. **Exclusive VIP Workbook** to guide you step-by-step as you implement what you've learn at the event.
2. Access to my **"How to Start Over" Digital Masterclass**, packed with insights, tools, and strategies to fuel your transformation journey.
3. A **One-on-One Virtual Coaching Session** with one of our featured authors, who will help you navigate your own personal comeback story.
4. Lifetime access to the **"START OVER" Community**, where you'll fnd ongoing inspiration, resources, and connections to keep you on track.

This event isn't just a ticket—it's an investment in the next, most extraordinary chapter of your life.

☞ **To claim your free ticket,** scan the QR code. Secure your spot now, as space is extremely limited at these events!

☞ **Collect all 10 books in the series *and* attend a live event to be in with a chance of winning an incredible £100K Prize Fund to help you 'Start Over'!**

If you:

- Purchase all 10 books in the series (and send us proof of purchase) and
- Attend a live event (and upload a selfe of you with Marco along with the hashtag #SOwithmarco to instagram)
- Email admin@marcorobinson.com to let us know you want to pitch!
- And you'll be invited to send us a video to tell us about the idea you have for a transformational business you'd like to start to help others through the same challenge you've overcome.
- Marco will select his favourite 10 pitches and invite them to the second round!
- If selected you'll pitch to Marco in person and ONE lucky winner will win our incredible 100k 'Start Over' prize package!

Here's how it works :

💡 Grand Prize: **£50K cash + £50K mentoring** (one winner)

💡 Runner-Up Prizes:

- Two x **£10K cash grants** (two winners)
- **£1K raffe at every live event** (must be in the room to win).

🔥 **BE QUICK THOUGH! LIMITED SEATS ARE AVAILABLE AT EACH EVENT!**

There are only 50 Free Seats Available at each live event so be quick and book yourself in as soon as you receive your free ticket. ***You need to be in the room to be in with a chance of winning both the raffe for 1k AND to get your selfe for the Pitch!*** 🔥

Don't Miss the Podcast & VIP Newsletter

🎙**Subscribe to the "HOW TO BE A HERO IN REAL LIFE" Podcast**

Dive deeper into the "START OVER" journey with behind-the-scenes stories, actionable strategies, and interviews with the remarkable authors featured in this series. Every episode is designed to give you the tools and inspiration to rise above challenges and build a life you're proud of.

Please scan the QR code subscribe to the podcast:

Join the VIP Newsletter List

Be the frst to hear about upcoming books, events, and exclusive offers. Plus, get access to bonus resources and transformational tips straight to your inbox. Subscribers are VIPs in the "START OVER" movement, receiving insights, updates, and tools to help you on your path.

Scan the QR code

Your Comeback Starts Now

You've read the stories. You've seen the proof. Now, it's your turn. Don't let this book be the end—make it the beginning. Start your sensational comeback today by:

1. **Pre-ordering the next edition of "START OVER."**
2. **Claiming your FREE ticket** to one of my life-changing live events.
3. **Subscribing to the podcast and VIP newsletter** for ongoing support and tools.

Your journey is just beginning. The rest of your life is waiting for you to rise, rebuild, and **become the hero of your own story.**

With unwavering belief in your power to rise, **Sir Marco Robinson**

Marco Robinson is an international #1 bestselling author, award-winning entrepreneur, and Top #2 Netfix producer. Renowned for creating and hosting Channel 4's prime-time TV show "Get a House for Free", where he gave homes to homeless families, Marco is a philanthropist knighted in the Commonwealth for his extraordinary charity work. A three-time winner of the prestigious Two Comma Club Award for generating millions in sales, Marco has built his legacy by inspiring people worldwide to turn loss into a sensational comeback. As the visionary behind the Start Over book series, he proves that no setback is too great to overcome.

Printed in Dunstable, United Kingdom

77352705R00178